WORDS
WORDS
WORDS

WORDS WORDS WORDS

David Crystal

OXFORD
UNIVERSITY PRESS

OXFORD

UNIVERSITY PRESS

Great Clarendon Street, Oxford OX2 6DP

Oxford University Press is a department of the University of Oxford.
It furthers the University's objective of excellence in research, scholarship,
and education by publishing worldwide in

Oxford New York

Auckland Cape Town Dar es Salaam Hong Kong Karachi
Kuala Lumpur Madrid Melbourne Mexico City Nairobi
New Delhi Shanghai Taipei Toronto

With offices in

Argentina Austria Brazil Chile Czech Republic France Greece
Guatemala Hungary Italy Japan Poland Portugal Singapore
South Korea Switzerland Thailand Turkey Ukraine Vietnam

Oxford is a registered trade mark of Oxford University Press
in the UK and in certain other countries

Published in the United States
by Oxford University Press Inc., New York

British Library Cataloguing in Publication Data
Data available

Library of Congress Cataloging in Publication Data
Data available

Typeset by Paul Saunders
Printed in Great Britain
on acid-free paper by Clays Ltd, St Ives plc

ISBN 0-19-861444-6
ISBN 978-0-19-861444-9

1 3 5 7 9 10 8 6 4 2

Contents

Preface

I can distinctly remember the day I first got interested in words. I think I must have been about three or four—certainly it was well before I went to school. It was in my home town of Holyhead, in North Wales. I was with some other kids, I don't know why, perhaps a playgroup of some kind, and the person looking after us had been calling us 'children', when she wanted to talk to us all. Then at one point she called us 'plant'. 'Nawr plant . . . ', she said.

It was, of course, Welsh, though I didn't know it at the time. 'Nawr plant' means 'Now, children'. But I recall being puzzled. I knew what a plant was. It was a green sort of thing that grew in gardens and in pots. Why were we being called green things that grow in pots? I couldn't work it out.

Welsh wasn't the language of our home, so I asked Uncle Joe about it. He was a Welsh speaker. He told me that 'plant' meant 'children'—and then, perhaps sensing an interest, he went on to tell me that my name was 'Dafydd' in Welsh. I took it in avidly. So I had *two* first names. That sounded interesting. But there was more. 'Dafydd y Garreg Wen', he called me, playfully, glossing it as 'David of the White Rock'. I had no idea who this was, but it sounded wonderful.

Then I went to school, and learned that Dafydd was the hero of an old Welsh folksong. I learned Welsh alongside English, and Welsh English alongside English English. And Irish English too, for this was Holyhead, and Dublin was only sixty-odd miles away. And my mother's side of the family were Irish, so that meant trips to County Wexford, where they spoke strangely. And some there spoke yet another language, which I would later come to know as Gaelic. And in church there was something else, called Latin. Was there no end to this language business?

Words, Words, Words

Sixty-two years later, and I know the study of language, and of languages, has no end. Although all the world's 6,000 or so languages have fascinated me, it is English with which I have had the most intense love-affair, probably because of its literature. And within English, it has been the words, words, words, in their thousands, which have most intrigued me. Words, and especially the way they sound. I don't know why that original sense of childish wonderment never left me, but it didn't. I can still stand open-mouthed in delight at a novel use of a word, just as I did all that time ago.

People love to share their interests with each other, and I am no exception. I read as many books as I can on language, and write them as often as I can. I never travel anywhere without a notebook for jotting down language observations. My office overflows with newspaper cuttings. The digital camera has been a boon for taking a quick shot of an interesting street sign. *International Shoppes* I saw recently at an airport: the modern world curiously juxtaposed against ye olde worlde.

No book on words could ever be comprehensive, but it can at least be representative of what is 'out there'. Language is too huge a subject to be discovered by any one person. Everyone has their own linguistic story to tell, and each story is worth the telling. *Words*, *Words*, *Words* is part of *my* story, a cross-section of my lexical autobiography.

David Crystal

Part I

The universe of words

We map out the universe of words. Chapter 1 explores the mind and motivation of wordsmiths. Why are people so fascinated by words? The answers take us into the distant past and around the globe. Chapter 2 debates the size of this universe. Is it possible to estimate how many words there are in a language? Can we put a figure on the number that exist in English? The total turns out to be remarkably large. Chapter 3 reports on the way children learn vocabulary, and investigates just how many words adults eventually learn. That total also turns out to be remarkably large. Chapter 4 explores the way vocabulary is organized. The apparently simple task of learning a new word makes us reflect on the way we group words into fields of meaning, and draws our attention to the central role of definitions in the use of language. Part I then concludes with a bow in the direction of the professional wordsmiths, the lexicographers, whose mission is to boldly go exploring all parts of the universe of words.

1 **Wordsmithery**

We live in a universe of words, and we know it. We even have names for those who are aware that they live in this universe and who have become mildly or seriously obsessed by it. We call them wordsmiths, word-buffs, wordaholics. We feed their obsession by publishing books of wordgames, putting word-puzzles in newspapers, playing wordgames on radio or television, and setting up word websites. There are now thousands of places on the Internet where they can indulge themselves. World Wide Web was a misnomer. It should have been Word Wide Web.

My pronouns are wrong. *We* call *them* wordsmiths? There is no 'us' and 'them' in the universe of words. We are all wordsmiths. I have never met anyone without an interest in words. For some, it is the words that turn up in a local dialect. Or the curious formations that their children invent. Or the new words they meet when they travel abroad. Or the unusual history of a word's meaning. Or a word they especially like or dislike. Or the meaning of their name, or their child's name, or the name of the place where they live. For most of us, it is all of these things, and much more besides.

Wordsmithery—or lexicology, as linguists call it—is a fascination that demands regular and repeated treatment. There are so many words that no one book or broadcast can deal with everything. And even if, through some magic, it was possible to present an account of all the words in a language today, the book would be out-of-date by tomorrow. Language changes. Words change. Our feelings about words change. And not just over long periods of time. It need only take a day. On 3 October 1957, ask anyone what a 'sputnik' was, and they would have been mystified. A day later, the word was on everyone's lips. These days, of course, the Internet can send a new word around the world in a matter of minutes.

3

Ground zero obtained a new global lease of life by the evening of September 11 2001.

Where does this fascination with words come from? Its roots lie deep in the history of the human race. The 'naming of parts' is there from the outset, according to the Genesis story in the Bible: 'and whatever the man called every living creature, that was its name'. Nor is this unique to the Bible. Many cultures have a word-myth as part of their origins. Words are perceived as special, magical, sacred—and personal names even more so. In the beginning, it seems everywhere, was the word.

The special role and power of words has been acknowledged throughout history by poets, philosophers, and proverbialists. By Confucius: 'He who does not understand words, cannot understand people'. By Aristophanes: 'Words can give everybody wings'. By Walt Whitman: 'Nothing is more spiritual than words'. And, as if to emphasize the darker side of the word universe, there is Lord Byron's couplet in *Lara*:

> Religion—freedom—vengeance—what you will,
> A word's enough to raise mankind to kill.

Words: for and against

The paradoxes presented by words are well represented in any selection of the world's proverbs.

Proverbs in favour of words

A word is medicine to the wise. (Telugu)
Words have no boundaries. (Bulgarian)
Words are sounds of the heart. (Chinese)
Words will endure; ways will fall into disuse. (Tamil)
There is nothing one goes to meet with more pleasure than the word. (Rwandan)
A word spoken at the right moment is like a golden apple on a silver dish. (Silesian)

Proverbs against words

Words and feathers are tossed by the wind. (Spanish)
The poison of a word is a word. (Swahili)
Cloth shrinks, words still more. (Russian)
A good word does much, but doesn't fill the fasting. (Norwegian)
Words are but sands; 'tis money buys lands. (Italian)
Words are good, but hens lay eggs. (German)

A recurrent literary theme is the danger of words. Words as misleaders.
Words as smokescreens. Words as weapons. They have been compared to
drugs and arrows, bullets and cannonballs. They are said to hurt, pierce,
stab, sting, and kill. They can, of course, also calm, soothe, and heal. It is
the potential force behind words which most impresses the world's writers.
And the world's criminals. 'Words are the new weapons', says Elliott Carver,
the manipulative media baron in the James Bond film *Tomorrow Never Dies*.
But Shakespeare was there first. 'She speaks poniards', says Benedick of
Beatrice, 'and every word stabs' (*Much Ado About Nothing*, 2.1.231).

And yet there is a paradox, for another great theme in literature is the
emptiness of words. Words by themselves do nothing. 'What is honour?',
asks Falstaff in *Henry IV Part 1* (5.1.133). And he answers himself:
'A word. What is that word, honour? Air.' Words are indeed, at one level,
just mouthfuls of air. In *Troilus and Cressida* (3.2.54), Pandarus harangues
Troilus for his tentative approach to Cressida: 'Words pay no debts; give
her deeds.' And in modern times, the US politician Adlai Stevenson
provided a caustic summary: 'Man does not live by words alone, despite
the fact that sometimes he has to eat them'.

Additionally, we have the aesthetic dimension. Words have been
compared to gems, leaves, flowers, sunbeams, lamps, thunder. One of the
best ever descriptions of the beauty of words was made by the novelist
Rose Macaulay in 1935, in her essay on 'Writing' in *Personal Pleasures*:

> Words, those precious gems of queer shape and gay colours, sharp
> angles and soft contours, shades of meaning laid one over the other

down history, so that for those far back one must delve among the lost and lovely litter that strews the centuries. They arrange themselves in the most elegant odd patterns; they sound the strangest sweet euphonious notes; they flute and sing and taber, and disappear, like apparitions, with a curious perfume and a most melodious twang.

Perhaps it is the paradoxical love-hate relationship we have with words which adds to their fascination. Or perhaps it is their schizophrenic character, so tangible in writing and so evanescent in speech. How are we to handle entities which have such multiple personalities? Do we let them control us or do we try to control them? Lewis Carroll's Humpty Dumpty, in a famous quotation from chapter 6 of *Through the Looking Glass* (1871), was in no doubt:

> 'When I use a word,' Humpty Dumpty said, in rather a scornful tone, 'it means just what I choose it to mean—neither more nor less.'
> 'The question is,' said Alice, 'whether you *can* make a word mean so many different things.'
> 'The question is,' said Humpty Dumpty, 'which is to be master—that's all.'

So how do we become 'masters of words'?

My answer is simple: by studying them. Words are a bit like children: we need to know how to look after them and when to let them look after themselves; when to be proud of them, and when to be worried about them. To do all that, we need to find out as much as we can about them. We need to know which are the dangerous words, because they mislead or confuse—what are sometimes called 'weasel words'. We need to know which words are ambiguous, which are loaded, which are clear. We need to know how words change their meanings and uses, and why. We need to understand the communicative properties of words, so that we can exploit them to our advantage. Above all, we need to be able to describe, comprehensively and objectively, the universe of words, and the way people live in it. In short, we need to become lexicologists.

Lexicology is the study of words, and this book is about lexicology. To be more precise, it is chiefly about the lexicology of English—the language which has the largest and most diverse wordstock of any of the world's languages because of its global spread and—as we shall see in chapter 8—the welcoming attitude displayed by its speakers towards the foreign words they encounter. Although I shall make some references to other languages, there is more than enough to do concentrating on English.

404 Error

Everyone logged on to the Internet will have encountered this message sooner or later. A 'four-oh-four' error. It tells you that your browser has made a faulty request to a server, typically because a page or site no longer exists. But why 404? The expression derives from the 'file not found' message sent out as a response to a faulty enquiry by staff at CERN, in Switzerland—the place where the World Wide Web was devised. The members of staff worked out of room 404.

Extended uses of the word soon followed, especially in the spoken language of the computer fraternity. As an adjective, applied to humans, it came to mean 'confused, blank, uncertain':

> *You've got a 404 look on your face*
> (or 'stupid, uninformed, clueless').
> *You'll never get an answer from that 404 headcase*
> (or 'unavailable, not around').
> *Jane's 404* (i.e. not at her desk).

And as a verb, it began to mean 'make no progress':

> *I'm 404-ing on that new code.*

The error message continues to appear on our screens, so we cannot ignore it. We can therefore expect more uses to emerge, as time goes by. And to see it in dictionaries. (It has already been logged for inclusion by the *Oxford English Dictionary*.)

The universe of words

Just as zoology is the study of all animals, so lexicology is the study of all words. That means, in the case of English, the words of all dialects and styles, whoever uses them and wherever they live. Over 1,500 million people use English around the world, in all kinds of varied and unpredictable lexical ways. Part of the joy of lexicology is to discover this unpredictability, region by region, in much the same way as an unexpected colour or fragrance delights us as we round a corner in a botanical garden. To study only the vocabulary of the variety known as standard English would be to miss out on many wonders of the lexical world. Some of the most interesting things that happen to words are to be found in the dialects and slang that make up non-standard English.

There is a danger in word-books. It is easy to slip into a style which presents long lists, of the kind: 'English has borrowed many words from French, and here are twenty-six of them, from A to Z.' Lists can be useful, but they are not the best way into a language's lexicon. Rather, we need to focus on general patterns and trends, such as the importance of diversity, change, creativity, and play in the way words are used. But if you are a true wordsmith, you will not be satisfied even with general themes. You will want to investigate individual word-stories. The real fascination of lexicology lies in the exploration of individual cases. Behind each name in the telephone directory is a unique person, any one of whose life stories is—as Dr Johnson once remarked—well worth the telling. It is the same with the biography of words.

2 Wordhoards

The Anglo-Saxon poet-singers used to talk of their 'wordhoard'. They were thinking of the collection of words they held in their head, which they could draw upon when they were performing. Heroes have wordhoards too. Beowulf, at one point in the great Anglo-Saxon epic (line 259), *wordhord anleac*—'unlocked his wordhoard'—and makes a speech. We do the same today. Inside each brain is a wordhoard, always changing, always growing. In fact, three-quarters of the human race have *two* wordhoards: we call such people 'bilingual'. Some have three or more. There seem to be no limits, other than those imposed by time, opportunity, and motivation, to the number of language and dialect vocabularies we can learn.

Of course, no one person knows the entire vocabulary of a language. That is a composite, comprising the wordhoards of each of us as individuals, and reflecting our regional, social, and professional backgrounds. There is a large number of words that everyone knows, but these are far outnumbered by the words that only a relatively few people know—such as all the technical terms of chemistry, law, engineering, medicine, and sumo wrestling. Four-fifths of the vocabulary of English has a highly restricted circulation. Most of it, like the bulk of an iceberg, lies beneath the surface of everyday usage, unseen and unnoticed by all but specialists—and passing lexicologists.

So, how large is the lexicon? One of the most popular questions lexicologists get asked is 'how many words are there in English?' It seems like a question which should have a very simple answer, but it turns out to be surprisingly difficult to arrive at even an approximate figure—for any language. If we go on a short lexiquest, we soon see why.

We can begin the journey by looking at a dictionary or two. What figure would we come up with if we counted the words listed in the largest dictionaries? *The Oxford English Dictionary* (usually referred to as 'the OED') had over 500,000 entries in its 1992 edition. *The Third New Webster International* ('W3', for short), the largest American dictionary, had over 450,000 entries when it was published in 1961. Although both dictionaries have grown since, that sounds as if there are around half a million words in English.

But if we were to compare the listings in these two huge works, we would find that they were not the same. The OED, for example, contains a large number of entries from earlier periods in the history of the language, which are outside the remit of W3. American dictionaries include more names of people and places. And the two works take different views about the range of dialect or technical terms they include. I once looked at all the words beginning with *sa-* in the OED and W3, and found that only about a third of them were in both books. Other samples produced similar results. So, if we were to make a 'superdictionary' by combining the lexicons contained in the two dictionaries, it rather looks as if our total would point steadily towards a million.

But our numerical lexiquest does not stop there. I have on my shelves a dictionary of the English used in South Africa. I have another of the English used in Jamaica. The first has over 3,000 entries; the second has around 15,000. Most of the words do not appear in either the OED or W3—or, for that matter, in any of the other dictionaries you would find routinely in a British or American bookstore. There is no reason why they should. Words which are used only in South Africa are presumably of limited interest to people living elsewhere. But they are nonetheless a part of the English language. And when we take into account all the parts of the world where English is spoken, and think of all the regional vocabulary encountered there (see chapter 14), we can sense immediately that this dimension will add hundreds of thousands more words to our language total.

We are well over a million now, yet still other lexical horizons are in view. What, to begin with, are we to do with all the abbreviations made up of initial letters—the *acronyms* of the language? Do these count as words?

Comparing lexicons

Here is a small sample from the beginning of letter S, derived from W3 and the OED. Of the twenty words shown, only five are in both works.

Word	In W3?	In OED?
saba	yes	no
sabadilla	yes	yes
sabadillia	no	yes
sabadilline	no	yes
sabadine	yes	yes
sabadinine	yes	no
sabaean	yes	yes
sabahdaur	no	yes
sabai grass	yes	no
sabaism	no	yes
sabakha	yes	no
sabal	yes	yes
sabalo	yes	yes
sabalote	yes	no
sabal palmetto	yes	no
sabana	yes	no
sabaoth	no	yes
sabarcane	no	yes
sabate	no	yes
sabatia	no	yes

You can do this exercise yourself, using any two dictionaries of roughly the same size. It is a good way of learning about their strengths and biases.

If I say *The BBC and CNN both reported the story*, may I say that there are eight words in this sentence? The point seems uncontentious. The fact that I've said *BBC* rather than *British Broadcasting Corporation* is almost incidental—more to do with linguistic energy-saving than anything else. Three syllables roll off the tongue, or pen, or keyboard more smoothly than nine.

But there are a lot of acronyms in English. The Gale *Acronyms, Initialisms and Abbreviations Dictionary* contains well over half a million entries, and is by no means a complete guide. They go from such items as AAAA (standing for the American Association of Advertising Agencies and over a dozen other organizations) to ZZZZ (an abbreviation used in aviation code, referring to unknown elements in a flight plan). In a recent edition, there were over 200 entries for the acronym PA alone. Including all these in our wordhoard would make it grow significantly towards two million.

And there is more. What about all the names of people and places in the English-speaking world—the 'proper names', as grammars call them. Should we include in our wordhoard for English such items as *Liverpool* and *Himalayas* and *Darth Vader*? Here, the instinct is to say no. These entities exist outside of language, in the sense that no one language 'owns' them. Darth Vader is Darth Vader, albeit in differing pronunciations, in English, French, Swahili, and Chinese. No one would ever include such words in a language total. If we wanted to find out what Darth Vader 'meant', we would look him up in an encyclopedia, not in a dictionary. And the same goes for Liverpool and the Himalayas. An old music-hall joke makes the point:

> *Bill*: I say, I say, I say, I can speak French.
> *Ben*: I didn't know you could speak French. Let me hear you speak French.
> *Bill*: Paris, Marseilles, Nice, Charles de Gaulle . . .

But if we are to exclude these names, why do I say 'there is more'? Because quite a few proper names take on a more general meaning; and

specifications

Cabinet

Intel® Pentium® 4 pro

Memory (RAM)

Hard Drive

DVD-ROM

DVD+-RW

11-in-1 media bay reader

Graphics card

Analogue video in/out

USB 2.0 ports

Firewire ports

Sound

peakers

modem

these we *would* want to include in our wordhoard total. Think of *Whitehall* and the *White House*—both proper names of places. There is nothing linguistically interesting about the street and the building, as such, but if I were to say *Several unusual signals have come out of Whitehall this week*, something different is happening. I do not mean that we have seen blue traffic lights at the junction of Whitehall and Trafalgar Square. Rather, by Whitehall I am referring to the presence of the Civil Service, which has some of its central offices along the street. Likewise, personal names can convey general associations: *That's a very Alf Garnett kind of remark*, someone might say after hearing a racist comment.

How many proper names are there which work in this way? Nobody knows. The names vary greatly from country to country. The Alf Garnett remark would be intelligible in the UK, where people are likely to remember the TV sitcom 'Till Death Us Do Part', which introduced us to this character. By contrast, the allusion would mean very little in the US. The equivalent personage there is Archie Bunker, a character from the 1970s TV series 'All in the Family'. Similarly, the seedy sexual connotations which attach to *Soho* in London do not travel along with the name. There is no corresponding set of associations surrounding the district of *SoHo* in New York City. And the sentences one might say about *King's Cross* in London do not transfer to *King's Cross* in Sydney—or of course vice versa.

Our lexiquest is not over yet. There are, I am reliably informed, over a million species of insects and other tiny animals so far identified in our world. Each has a name. Admittedly, the name might be in Latin, or in a loanword approximation to Latin, but that does not stop me speaking or writing the following English sentence: *Araneae, Acari, and Scorpiones are included in the class Arachnida*. Or, in more popular language: 'spiders, ticks and mites, and scorpions are included in the class of arachnids.' There are as many names for things as there are things which have been discovered, whether we are talking about botanical species or chemical compounds. We must not exclude these from our total. The beauty of language is that it allows us to talk about anything we want to.

What do these names mean?

All of these place names have a more general meaning. The task is to establish which meaning goes with which name. It is not difficult to do this for the names belonging to one's own culture; it is harder to do it for other parts of the English-speaking world, unless the name has 'travelled'. (*Answers*: p. 207)

Name	Associated meaning
Broadway	advertising
Number 10	policing
Madison Avenue	justice
Bollywood	security
Fleet Street	UK government
Old Bailey	medicine
Harley Street	newspaper publishing
Fort Knox	prison
Dartmoor	theatre world
Scotland Yard	films

At the end of our lexiquest, our total now hovers uncertainly in the millions. If we exclude all the abbreviations, proper names, and really esoteric technical terms, we are down to around one million. Excluding all the regional dialectisms and historically obsolescent words would take the total down to less than half a million. There is no single answer. Perhaps the best response to the question 'how many words are there in English?' is to say simply 'a lot', and move on. There are far more interesting questions to explore—such as how many of these words does the average person know? And how do we come to learn them in the first place? We must begin our wordhoard enquiry with the child.

Words about words

In all the examples so far, I have assumed that we all know what a 'word' is. And in written English, for the most part, we do know. A word is something with a space on either side. *There are eight words in the present sentence.*

If it were as easy as that, lexicology would soon get boring. Fortunately, it isn't. The identity of words poses several intriguing problems. Answer me this: how many words are there in the following sentence?

I put the flower-pot on the washing-machine.

I assume you will have thought seven. But what if I had written the sentence like this?

I put the flower pot on the washing machine.

Will you now say there are nine words there? And yet the two sentences mean the same thing. All that has changed is a pair of hyphens.

Say the sentence out loud. There are no spaces or hyphens now. *Flower-pot* is plainly a single word, even though it has two parts. It refers to one object, after all, not two. Such words are called *compounds*, and we shall look at them again in chapter 9. In writing, some compounds have three shapes: we can write *flower pot* (spaced), *flower-pot* (hyphenated), or *flowerpot* (solid). Word counting starts to get tricky under these conditions. When you see two words, they sometimes count as one.

And what about this further complication? How many different words are there in this list?

I walk. He walks. She is walking. They walked.

There are plainly nine words here, but are they all 'different' words? At one level they are: they look different. But are they different in meaning? If you were learning English as a foreign language, you would have to learn *I*, *he*, *she*, *is*, and *they*, but what about the remaining four? Would you feel that *walk*, *walks*, *walking*, and *walked* were four different words?

The answer, of course, is no. We would say that here we have four forms, or variants, of the one word WALK. *I walk*, we would say, is the 'present tense' of WALK; *They walked* is the 'past tense'; and so on. They are grammatically different forms of the same entity. So, despite the fact that we see four words, there is really only one. One unit of sense. Linguists have a term for this unit: they call it a *lexeme*. *Walk*, *walks*, *walking*, and *walked*, they would say, are variants of the lexeme WALK.

This isn't just a theoretical issue, of no practical consequence. Whether you count words or count lexemes makes a huge difference. How many 'different words' are there in Shakespeare, for instance? If we count all the word variants as separate words, we get over 30,000. If we count just the lexemes, and ignore all the variants, we get less than 20,000.

3 **Wordgrowth**

The 'first word' is a major step forward in a child's development, and parents look forward to it eagerly. But they are often surprised by what they hear. Though they might confidently expect it to be *mummy* **or** *daddy***, it just as often turns out to be** *teddy* **or** *drink* **or** *peep-bo* **or** *ooh***. They shouldn't get upset. Babies, like adults, tend not to talk about the obvious, but to comment on what is novel or dramatic. It isn't just teenagers who think that there are more interesting things in life than parents.**

It all happens around twelve months of age. That is the usual date of appearance for the 'first word'. Some children have been heard to articulate a clear word as early as eight or nine months. Many leave it until a lot later, sometimes as late as two, and they then catch up rapidly. A few have problems of language development, and need special help before their word learning progresses.

Some leave out the first-word stage completely and launch themselves directly into simple sentences. Lord Macaulay, the historian, is said to have been a very late talker. There's a story told about him that, when his language finally emerged around age three, he was asked why his first words had come so late, to which he is supposed to have replied: 'Hitherto, nothing of sufficient significance has warranted my verbal attention'. You may be forgiven scepticism!

Whenever it appears, the first word is soon followed by others. Between twelve and eighteen months, most children produce around fifty words. In one study, the average time it took them to get from ten to fifty words was 4.8 months—that is, about ten new words a month. Between eighteen months and two years, the rate increases to about twenty-five a month.

It then becomes much more difficult to count word growth. By two, active vocabulary has grown to around 200 words. By three, the figure is somewhere between 3,000 and 5,000. One study recorded a child at age three years and six months for a whole day and counted up all her words. She produced 37,000 words in total, and over 4,000 different words. At times she was talking at a rate of a hundred words a minute.

The totals seem remarkable until you actually spend some time listening to an articulate four-year-old, and find yourself wishing they would shut up so that you can get a word in! Remember also that it does not take long to say 1,000 words. That's the number we would expect to find in a five-minute conversation. Even at a staid pace, such as that used by a radio newsreader, more linguistic ground is covered than you might think: a news bulletin is usually read at around 200 words a minute.

If children can produce up to fifty words by eighteen months (their *active* vocabulary), how many can they understand (their *passive* vocabulary)? This is a more difficult area to research, but the studies show that progress here is even more impressive. During those first months of the second year, children are homing in on new words at over twenty each month—nearly one a day. By eighteen months, most children understand around 250 words. It seems that for every one word they can speak, they understand five.

Children's early words

The words children use in their second year are mainly about the 'here and now' of what is happening around them. If you keep a diary, you will find that it is possible to group them into different fields of meaning (p. 29) that the children want to talk about. It doesn't take long before there are words belonging to the following fields. (Of course, they will not all be pronounced in an adult way, at this stage.)

- people: *mummy, daddy, grandad, milkman, baba, Mikey, Sue* (or whatever the siblings' names are)

- actions: *bye-bye, hello, upsy-daisy, all gone, fall down, night-night*
- food: *milk, juice, drink, cookie, banana, din-din*
- body parts and functions: *mouth, nose, eyes, hands, toes, wee-wee, pooh*
- clothing: *hat, nappy (diaper in the US), shoes, pyjamas, coat*
- animals and their noises: *dog(gie), cat, pussy, bird(ie), moo, baalamb, woof*
- vehicles and their noises: *car, truck, train, bus, brm, beep-beep*
- toys and games: *ball, bricks, book, doll(y), clap hands, peep-bo* (in the UK; *peek-a-boo*, especially in the US)
- household objects and their noises: *cup, spoon, plate, bottle, brush, light, clock, tick-tock*
- locations: *look, there, in, on, that, mine*
- social words: *yes, no, please, ta, want*
- describing words: *hot, nice, pretty, big*

It is a ratio which reduces gradually as children get older, but the imbalance between active and passive vocabulary remains with us for the rest of our lives. As adults, our passive vocabulary is usually a third larger than our active vocabulary. We understand far more words than we routinely use. Apart from in this example, I do not think I have ever used the word *telemetry* in my life. I am not even sure where the stressed syllable goes: is it *telemetry* or *telemeetry*? But I know what it means.

How can we find out what our active and passive levels are? Most people are intrigued by the question, and would like to know how large their wordhoard is. One method of calculation is therefore given at the back of the book (*see* 'Becoming a word detective', 4). But if you try it out, be prepared for surprises. Virtually everyone thinks their total is smaller than in fact it is. I asked a group of people to guess at the number of words they actively used. The answers ranged from 5,000 to 20,000. The second figure is nearer the truth, but it is still only half the truth.

It is unusual to find someone with an active vocabulary of less than 35,000 words, and a passive vocabulary of less than 50,000. For someone who has been through higher education, who mixes in literate circles, and who reads a lot, the levels are twice as high. A passive vocabulary of 100,000 words? It sounds a great deal, until we realize that the typical 'concise' dictionary—a book of 1,500 pages or so—contains around 100,000 entries. And if you scan the entries, in the manner of 'Becoming a word detective', you will find that you know at least half of them, and (for readers of this book, who doubtless have a special interest in words) probably a great deal more than that.

We always underestimate vocabulary size. Sometimes we stereotype people as having small vocabularies. It is widely believed that there are languages in the world which have only a few hundred words—the aboriginal languages of Australia are often cited. This is nonsense. Regardless of the so-called 'primitiveness' of the people (as judged by Western standards), the languages they speak display a level of growth and complexity quite comparable to those we associate with the more 'advanced' societies. And it is the same with readers of *The Sun* newspaper.

The Sun rises unexpectedly at this point because it has received so much unfair linguistic stereotyping. 'The average *Sun* reader', I heard a television pundit once say, 'has a vocabulary of less than 500 words'. It is a comment, indirectly, on the supposed lack of linguistic sophistication of the tabloid press. When people see headlines in non-standard spelling or grammar, such as GOTCHA! or WE AIN'T LEAVING, they assume—wrongly—that the writers are linguistically deficient. But just because people say *ain't* tells us nothing about how much vocabulary they know. And in the case of *The Sun*, the vocabulary levels are much higher than people think.

I spent an interesting day in 2003 counting all the words in 100 articles taken from an online edition of *The Sun*. That is not as sad as it sounds.

A colleague wrote a computer program which extracted all the words, removed duplicates, sorted them into alphabetical order, and did a count. It was by no means the whole newspaper (the advertisements, for example, do not appear online), but the total for that sample was 5,190 different words. It included words like *abdicate* and *abdominal* and *academic*—words that would be just as likely to turn up in *The Times*. If I had done the whole newspaper, I think the vocabulary for that one day would easily have reached 6,000, and probably 7,000.

Let us put that total in context. The number of different words in the King James Bible is around 8,000.

There are, unfortunately, people who do have a small vocabulary size. Language, as any other area of human development and behaviour, can be affected by disability, and vocabulary is often the main symptom. Children who suffer from delayed language development, or who have a language disorder, may end up with a very limited lexicon. I once worked with a seven-year-old boy, Sam, who had a total active vocabulary of only 200 words. At that age, it should have been somewhere between 5,000

Words in THE SUN

A selection of different words encountered in *The Sun* experiment, taken from the middle of the e's:

. . . email, embark, embarrass, embed, embezzle, embrace, embroider, emerge, emergency, emotion, emotional, emperor, empire, employ, employee, employer, emptiness, enable, enclose, encounter, encourage, end, endure, enema, enemy, energetic, energy, engage, engine, engineer, engineering, Englishman, enhance, enigmatically, enjoy, enjoyable, enlarge, enormous, enough, ensemble, ensuing, ensure, enter, entertain, entertainment, enthusiast, enthusiastic, entire, entirely, entrant, entry, envious, environment . . .

and 10,000. The focus of the work by his speech and language therapist was to increase this total, and she was having some success, but it was slow and painstaking, and required the help of all those with whom Sam came into contact. New words can easily be introduced in a half-hour clinical session, but to become part of a child's routine behaviour they need to be practised throughout the whole day, and that means bringing up linguistic reinforcements in the form of parents, teachers, siblings, shopkeepers, and anyone else who can provide lexical models to follow.

It isn't only children who may have a small vocabulary. Adults with learning disabilities typically operate with a very limited range. And people who have suffered a stroke or other brain damage can demonstrate one of the most poignant linguistic situations of all—the complete or near-complete loss of a previously well-developed vocabulary. It seems amazing that even a small brain haemorrhage can wipe out the active use of 50,000 words just like that. But if the damage directly affects that part of the brain which controls the production of speech, it can happen.

So how does one teach—or re-teach—vocabulary to someone who does not have it? How do we learn new words? The issues apply to many more than those who have suffered some form of language disability. They are questions that all teachers need to answer, when they introduce children to the intellectual universe of words. And they are questions that everyone is faced with when they encounter a previously unknown lexical domain within this universe, such as learning a foreign language, a new dialect, or a new subject area. The task of new word-learning is always with us, whether we are reading a novel, watching television, or grappling with a tax return form. There seems to be a drive within all of us to increase the size of our wordhoard. 'It pays to increase your word-power' was a famous *Reader's Digest* column. It's true. But how is it done?

4 **Wordfields**

It sounds very simple: teach a new word; learn a new word. But the task is more complex than it seems. To illustrate, let us learn one now.

If the exercise is to work for all readers, I have to find a word no one will have encountered before. To guarantee this I have to invent one. I therefore choose *debagonization*, created today for this book, at no extra charge, and I will not believe any readers who claim they have been using it for years.

Debagonization is actually a very important state, and I find it inexplicable that the word has not arrived in the language hitherto, as it affects all of us who have travelled by air. It is the cessation of anxiety when our luggage eventually emerges from the black hole of an airport carousel. Until that point we had been bagonizing, often for some time, when everyone else's luggage appeared, but not ours. We had worked ourselves up into a frenzy, believing that our bags were still in Barcelona. We were therefore in a state of bagonization. Then they appear. We are in that state no longer. And if we want to inform our fellow-travellers of our new state of mind, we now have a word for it.

So, we have all now learned a new word. Correction. We have all learned several new words. To explain *debagonization* I had to mention *bagonization*, and that in turn required a reference to *bagonize*. The constituents of *bagonize* you would already know: it is a clever blend (*see* chapter 9) of *bag* and *agonize*. *Bagonize* you might have encountered before, because I have been trying to get it into the language for years, and have mentioned it in lectures and other books. But I have never used the *-ization* form, until now.

The principle is plain: a new word depends on old ones for its meaning. 'Old' in the sense of 'familiar, known'. Let me repeat my definition:

> the cessation of anxiety when our luggage eventually emerges from the black hole of an airport carousel.

Leaving aside my cosmic metaphor, which is there to add drama more than clarity, I had to use seven specific elements to capture the exact sense: *cessation*, *anxiety*, *luggage*, *eventually*, *emerges*, *airport*, and *carousel*. My definition of course assumed a certain level of word knowledge on the part of my readership. Words like *cessation* are quite advanced. If I had assumed less knowledge—in trying to explain it to a child, for example—I might have defined it thus:

> the feeling you have when you stop worrying because you've seen your bags drop onto the moving track in the place where you arrive at an airport.

But to make it easier, I have had to make the definition longer. I have used eleven specific words this time: *feeling*, *stop*, *worrying*, *seen*, *bags*, *drop*, *moving*, *track*, *place*, *arrive*, and *airport*.

That is always the case. It takes more linguistic energy to make things easy to understand. And the process continues if even more ease is required. If my reader did not understand *airport*, for instance, I would have to say something like 'a place with facilities enabling passengers or cargo to be transported using aeroplanes'. Thirteen words instead of one. If I have to explain *aeroplanes*, it would be something like (I quote from one dictionary) 'an aircraft that is heavier than air, has non-rotating wings from which it derives its lift, and is mechanically propelled (e.g. by a propeller or jet engine)'.

But, you might say, why not just define aeroplanes simply as 'machines which fly'? Because that would not be a very good definition. Helicopters, gliders, hot-air balloons and several other things are machines which fly. The definition has to apply only to aeroplanes and not to any of the others, otherwise it would be ambiguous and could mislead.

We are always giving out misleading definitions, in everyday life. Usually it doesn't matter, because people make allowances and read in the missing information from their knowledge of the world around them. Or the approximation is enough. For instance, if you ask me what an *autogiro* is and I say 'it's a sort of helicopter', this isn't a very good definition but it might be enough to satisfy your curiosity. The conversation would then move on. If it doesn't satisfy you, you can press me for more information and, if I can't supply it, we can resort to the final court of appeal. We can look it up in a dictionary, if we have one handy. This doesn't often happen. Usually, the approximation will do.

But here's a case where the approximation didn't do. It was in a school, where seven-year-old Ellen told me that her mother 'worked in a factory'. As there were no factories nearby, I asked her teacher how this could be. The teacher had no idea. Later we asked the mother, who said she didn't work in a factory. Puzzlement all round.

I asked Ellen what a factory was, and she told me: 'It's a place where you make things'. How did she know? Mummy told me. So did she know the sort of things mummy made in the factory? Of course. Cakes and dinner and things. It was plain that Ellen was talking about the kitchen in her house.

We can reconstruct what must have happened. 'What's a factory, mummy?' asks Ellen one day, probably because she's just read the word or heard it on television. 'A place where you make things, darling', says busy, distracted mother. And Ellen makes a mental note.

The definition was misleading. A factory is not 'a place where you make things'. Putting it loosely, it is 'one or more large buildings where lots of people make lots of things for sale'. But how many of us could come up with something specific like that on the spur of the moment?

Teachers, of course, have to do this sort of thing routinely. Not for them, or for their students, the luxury of lax definition. Lax definitions lose marks in essays and exams. And, in the wider world, lax definitions can lose

Espresso • Mocha L

Hot Chocolate • T

Hot & Cold Sandwic

Baguette • Pitta Br

Panini • Fresh Falal

Snacks • Bakl

arguments, business deals, and friends. How often do we hear 'That's not what I meant' or 'We seem to be at cross-purposes'? The broadcasting philosopher C.E.M. Joad used to say, when he was asked a question: 'It all depends what you mean by . . . ' It does, indeed, all depend on what we mean. And what we mean ultimately comes down to definitions.

So, to think out a good definition of *aeroplane* we have to work out in advance the features of an aeroplane which differentiate it from all other types of flying machine. And that means gathering together the words which name these other machines. How many are there? And how will we define them, so that they are different from *aeroplane*? Suddenly, in investigating one word, we find ourselves investigating the meanings of a whole field of them. And that, indeed, is what this cluster of related words is technically called: a *semantic field*.

Learning vocabulary is always a matter of building up fields of words. And we do it by comparing words with other words. That is how parents teach children. 'Careful! That's the hot tap. Use the cold one.' Here the young child is being taught the opposites: *hot* versus *cold*. Thirty years later and the somewhat older child will have encountered thousands of similar conversations, but with more difficult words. 'Careful! That's the positive terminal; use the negative one.'

So how do we compare words? There are several ways, and I have just illustrated one of them: we explain one word by contrasting it with another. What is *positive*? Not *negative*. What is *hot*? Not *cold*. We call such pairs *opposites*, or *antonyms*, and the relationship between them, we say, is one of *antonymy*.

Another common way is to say that one word is the same as another. What is *oblivion*? *Forgetfulness*. What is *sodium chloride*? *Salt*. We call such words *synonyms*, and the relationship between them is one of *synonymy*.

A third way is to say that one word is included in another. What is a *tulip*? A kind of *flower*. What is a *snake*? A kind of *reptile*. The technical term for this relationship is not so well known: it is *hyponymy*. *Tulip* is a hyponym of flower. Snake is a hyponym of *reptile*.

Although hyponymy is not so well known, it is in fact a much more important way of comparing words than either synonymy or antonymy. The reason is that there are very few words in a language which are exact synonyms (like *autumn* in British English and *fall* in American English) or which are exact opposites of each other. Most words don't have opposites. What is the opposite of *Tuesday*, or *tent*, or *tennis*? It's a nonsensical question. But look in a dictionary, and you will find hyponyms everywhere. The definitions rely on hyponymy most of the time.

This is how we build up our semantic fields. We gather together all the words that have related senses, such as, in the field of flowers, *tulip* and *daffodil* and *primrose* and (from another angle) *red* and *yellow* and *green* and (from another angle) *stalk* and *leaf* and *stamen*. If we want to talk about flowers, we need to have at our disposal a wide range of such words. Combine these words one way, and we end up with a definition: 'A daffodil is a flower with a large yellow, bell-like head.' Combine them in another, and we end up with a vivid description: 'A host of golden daffodils.'

Notice I say 'if we want to talk about flowers'. There is a big difference between 'talking about' flowers and 'knowing all about' flowers. I can confidently say that an *agapanthus* is a flower, but I would not be able to identify one in a garden shop. If I were bluffing in a conversation, not wanting to show my ignorance, I might nod wisely when someone says 'I think agapanthuses are very pretty flowers, don't you?' But bluffing is dangerous behaviour. If we can't back up our knowledge of a word with a reasonably adequate definition, we can end up being caught out. 'David, fetch me an agapanthus from the other room, would you?' 'Ah . . . '

We have to be honest. Everyone bluffs with words some of the time. We use words whose meanings we only partly understand, and usually we get away with it, because conversational life is not one long mutual interrogation. But we should always try to do better than this. We need to semantically grow up. We should always aim to be able to prove to someone that we know what we mean, and that means being able to provide a definition upon request. Definitions lie at the heart of word study.

So who are the people who are good at making up definitions? They are called lexicographers.

Plough your own semantic field

Try working out a semantic field for yourself. Take a field you know well, such as fruit, furniture, road vehicles, or instruments of the orchestra. The first step is to collect as many words belonging to this field that you can think of, using a thesaurus or an encyclopedia or just your own general knowledge. Don't worry if you leave any out. Then give each a rough definition. Next, sharpen the definition by making it exclude the other words. When you've done a handful, compare your results with the definitions given in a dictionary.

For example, if you chose instruments of the orchestra, you would end up with a list of several dozen words, such as *flute*, *trumpet*, and *violin*. To distinguish these three, you might say:

> *flute*: a kind of woodwind instrument
> *trumpet*: a kind of brass instrument
> *violin*: a kind of stringed instrument

So far, so good. But as you bring in other instruments, these very general definitions will not serve:

> *flute*: a kind of woodwind instrument
> *clarinet*: a kind of woodwind instrument

Now you have to add the critical features which distinguish them. Something like this:

> *flute*: a woodwind instrument consisting of a long tube played by holding it horizontally across the mouth and blowing air through a side hole
> *clarinet*: a woodwind instrument consisting of a long tube played by holding it vertically with one end in the mouth and blowing air through a reed

But that second definition could apply to *oboe* as well. Now things are getting a bit technical. What's the difference? The clarinet uses a single reed, the oboe a double reed. The range of the instruments differs, and so does their timbre. That will have to be brought into the definition too. And so we will continue: we will need to note that the fingers cover holes in the instrument and press keys—in order to distinguish a clarinet from a recorder, which has no keys.

It's quite a task, thinking out all the attributes that actually define the words, and even dictionaries don't include everything. Dictionaries have limited space, and lexicographers are human. When you compare your results with those in your dictionary, don't be surprised if your own efforts are sometimes an improvement.

5 **Wordworks**

Lexicographers create definitions for a living. They do a great deal else, in compiling dictionaries, but that is their primary task. A good dictionary thrives on the brilliance of its definitions. They have to be clear, succinct, relevant, and discriminating. They can also be elegant, humorous, quirky, and memorable. Definitions, in short, involve imagination and creativity, just as any other literary genre. Several, indeed, have achieved fame. Extracts from famous dictionaries are present in books of quotations, sitting very comfortably alongside quotes from novelists, essayists, poets, and dramatists.

Dr Johnson, whose *Dictionary* of 1755 heralded the modern era of lexicography, famously defined the lexicographer as a 'harmless drudge'. It was a tongue-in-cheek definition, but it was nonetheless quite wrong. Drudgery? Yes, there are moments, usually in the middle of letter S, when you look out of the window at the sky and wish you were in Hawaii. But that goes with many a job. You have to have the right temperament to be a lexicographer. If the size of the task puts you off, you do something else with your life. 'A large work is difficult because it is large', said Johnson in his Preface. And that is precisely its appeal.

You will never be a lexicographer if you keep thinking: I have written 4,686 definitions and I have 154,378 to go. Lexicographers and encyclopedists have one thing in common: they have to focus on the entry of the moment. While I am writing the entry for *picaresque*, I must concentrate on that to the exclusion of all other words. I must forget about *picador*, which I was working on an hour ago, and not look ahead to *picayune*, which I might with good luck start before 6 o'clock. No, all my skills must be devoted to making the entry on *picaresque* the best possible entry in the history of the world. And the reason is simple. When my readers-of-the-future look up *picaresque*, they are not interested in *picador* or *picayune*, or any other word. They want *picaresque*. For that moment, their attention is totally focused on that particular word. And so must mine be.

If you have a deep interest in words, then the prospect of 'studying them all' is the most enticing of all opportunities. Each word is its own world, with a unique past, present, and future. For lexicographers, there are no more intriguing, challenging, and rewarding tasks than to explore a word's history, establish its current forms and senses, and capture novel trends in its usage. And the results of their work are extraordinarily seductive. 'Were I asked,' said Samuel Taylor Coleridge, 'what I deemed the greatest and most unmixt benefit, which a wealthy individual, or an association of

Famous definitions

Here are some dictionary definitions included in *The Oxford Dictionary of Quotations*.

From Johnson's *Dictionary* (1755):
>   *Dull*. To make dictionaries is dull work.
>   *Excise*. A hateful tax levied upon commodities.
>   *Lexicographer*. A writer of dictionaries, a harmless drudge.
>   *Oats*. A grain, which in England is generally given to horses, but in Scotland supports the people.
>   *Pension*. Pay given to a state hireling for treason to his country.

From Ambrose Bierce's *The Cynic's Word Book* (1906), better known as *The Devil's Dictionary*:
>   *Applause*. The echo of a platitude.
>   *Auctioneer*. The man who proclaims with a hammer that he has picked a pocket with his tongue.
>   *Patience*. A minor form of despair, disguised as a virtue.
>   *Peace*. In international affairs, a period of cheating between two periods of fighting.
>   *Saint*. A dead sinner revised and edited.

wealthy individuals, could bestow on their country and on mankind, I should not hesitate to answer.' And what was his answer? A dictionary.

Is the drudgery harmless? Hardly. A misleading or biased definition could cause a great deal of trouble. All lexicographers know how careful they have to be when defining the senses of sensitive words, especially offensive race-related words, such as *nigger*, or words which can be taken in different ways, such as *Jew*. Today the sensitive areas include gender, sexuality, and disability. And lexicographers know that there will be unease if they include certain types of words, such as obscenities or colloquialisms. But they have to include them, if they are doing their job properly.

When Webster's *Third New International Dictionary* appeared in 1961, it included *ain't*; the row over whether it should have been included lasted for decades. And when Eric Partridge published his *Dictionary of Slang and Unconventional English* in 1937, the inclusion of certain words beginning with *f* and *c* led to the book being banned from library shelves for years. A library might own a copy, but it would keep it out of sight in a back room, and if you asked to see it you were scrutinized as if you were a pervert.

Dictionary companies have even been taken to court for their definitions. Most cases have been by major companies anxious to defend a trademarked name against exploitation by other companies. They insist on the name's continued use with a capital letter, and demand that definitions identify company origins. A surprising number of words have developed contentious generic meanings: they include *aspirin*, *band-aid*, *escalator*, *filofax*, *frisbee*, *sellotape*, *thermos*, *tippex*, and *xerox*. And the problem facing the lexicographer is how to handle them. If it is everyday usage to say such things as *I have a new hoover: it's an electrolux*, then the dictionary, which records everyday usage, should include the generic sense. The principle has been tested several times in the courts, and the right of the dictionary-makers to include such usages is repeatedly upheld. But the decision still has to be made: when does a proprietary name develop a sufficient general usage to be safely called generic?

The universe of words

Why do people get so upset? It is because of the status which dictionaries have acquired over the course of the past 200 years. They are perceived to be arbiters of taste, courts of linguistic appeal, lexical bibles . . . the metaphors are multiple, but they all have one thing in common. Dictionaries are perceived to be authorities on usage, texts which teach the difference between lexical right and wrong. If a word, a spelling, a pronunciation, or a sense gets into the dictionary, then, in some mysterious way, it is felt to be authorized. 'It's in the dictionary', we say. And if it isn't in the dictionary it is somehow suspect. It will not, for example, count in Scrabble. Could there be any greater condemnation?

The feelings of subservience, faced with a dictionary, can be very strongly held. One of the most remarkable statements of self-subjection was made by the government minister Lord Chesterfield upon the publication of Johnson's *Dictionary*. Reflecting on the mess that he thought the English language had got into, he says:

> We must have recourse to the old Roman expedient in times of confusion, and chuse a dictator. Upon this principle, I give my vote for Mr. Johnson, to fill that great and arduous post, and I hereby declare, that I make a total surrender of all my rights and privileges in the English language, as a free-born British subject, to the said Mr. Johnson, during the term of his dictatorship. Nay more, I will not only obey him like an old Roman, as my dictator, but, like a modern Roman, I will implicitly believe in him as my Pope, and hold him to be infallible while in the chair.

Somewhat extreme, perhaps, but the sentiment is by no means obsolete. And it is understandable, when we consider why dictionaries evolved in the first place.

To see the point of dictionaries, you have to conceive of a world without them. Imagine a world where, if you encountered a new word in somebody's conversation or writing, you had to guess what it might mean, because there was nowhere to 'look it up'. You might decide to use it yourself, but you would have no idea whether you were using it in

36

exactly the same sense as your model. And if you ended up using it in a different way, that would be all right too, because there was no source around to tell you not to. You could even spell the word however you wanted. Nobody could say you were right or wrong.

For the first thousand years of the history of English, that is how it was. It was a world where language was under no central control. When Shakespeare wanted a word to express a particular idea, he had no reference books to help him. He—and other Elizabethan authors —simply made one up. And if several writers all wanted to express the same idea, there would be several versions of the 'same' word in circulation. So, to express the notion 'characterized by discord', we find one author using *discordful* in 1596, another using *discordous* in 1597, and Shakespeare using *discordant* at the beginning of *Henry IV Part 2*. This is the sort of confusion that Chesterfield was thinking of.

To begin with, there was no problem. When people live in small communities, speaking their own local dialect, and travelling little, there is no pressure to evolve a national way of speech. And the same applies to writing, where words, grammar, and spelling comfortably reflect local norms of speech. Only when written texts come to be widely read, and mutual intelligibility on a national scale becomes necessary, do we find people feeling the need to use language in an agreed manner. It is a slow process, reflecting the way a country develops a national identity and a centralized government. The emergence of printing, and the widespread distribution of books, is another critical factor. In the case of English, it took 400 years, from around 1400 to around 1800, to develop what we now call 'standard English'.

The eighteenth century changed everything. That was the century of manners, of correctness, of a more sharply defined class distinction. Language, as one of the most natural and widespread means of distinguishing 'us' from 'them', was a notable focus of attention, and all aspects were affected. The period between 1750 and 1770 brought the first really influential prescriptive grammar book (Bishop Lowth's, in 1762), the first dictionary of pronunciations (John Walker's, in 1763), and

Johnson's hugely influential *Dictionary*. The idea was to bring the language under control. From now on, people—if they wanted to be perceived as educated and to avoid social criticism—would have to spell words, use grammar, and select vocabulary in the same way. After those two decades, English language study was never the same again.

Vocabulary was especially affected. Johnson took great pains to let his readers know which words would be acceptable in polite society and which would not: *impartible*, he says, is 'elegant'; but *slippy* is 'a barbarous provincial word'. Judgements about usage have been a feature of all dictionaries since, though usually avoiding such personal, emotive labels. Modern dictionaries continue the tradition of social awareness when they label a word as 'taboo', 'informal', or 'derogatory', or as belonging to law, physics, or medicine. The usage labels in a dictionary are one of its most important features.

Dictionaries have evolved in many other ways. Definitions are still their life-blood, but in addition you are likely to get information about spelling variation, syllable division, pronunciation, word history, and information about usage. And, above all, you are likely to get evidence.

Evidence, evidence, evidence. You cannot have too much evidence. If one person claims that *debagonization* (*see* p. 25) is an English word, and another says it isn't, how do we resolve the matter? Look it up in the dictionary. But what if the dictionaries disagree (and they often do)? What do we do if one dictionary says that *yoghourt* is the preferred spelling, and another says it is *yogurt*? Scrabble enthusiasts know very well just how often such disagreements arise. Dictionaries at dawn!

Two thousand years ago, Horace gave an answer to the question in his *Art of Poetry*. It is all a matter of usage, he says, 'in whose power lies the arbitrament, the rule, and the standard of language.' But whereas in his day it was impossible to have more than a general impression of everyday usage, today it is possible to get evidence on a grand scale about how people use words. And extracts of this evidence are published in the dictionaries themselves, in the form of examples, or *quotations*—extracts of usage from the users themselves. Johnson was the first to do this in a truly systematic way for English, and lexicographers have assiduously been collecting quotations ever since—both for spoken and for written language. But Johnson could never have imagined the powerful collection methods that modern lexicographers use to provide the evidence for their judgements. Or the amazing sources of data there are these days—not least, the World Wide Web.

You can't beat a large collection of examples—linguists call it a *corpus*—to justify a decision about usage. It's the only way to resolve a difference of personal opinion. If I say that X is the case and you deny it, then to support my claim, all I have to do is demonstrate that I have a thousand examples of other people's usage in my favour, while you have none, or very few. Corpus evidence is what counts, as long as the corpus is large enough and representative of the language as a whole. It is the only way to answer such questions as: Do women use *super* more than men? Do Americans use *automobile* more than Britons? Is it *email* or *e-mail*? *conjurer* or *conjuror*? *shredded* or *shred*? Is *blonde* used for men as well as women? Is *gay* still used in its sense of 'lighthearted'?

But a corpus does more than resolve arguments. It helps lexicographers improve their grasp of how words work, and eventually we all benefit. For instance, there is something odd about the use of the word *aftermath* in this sentence, but what is it exactly?

Smith held a victory party in the aftermath of his election as leader.

You would not be helped if your dictionary told you (as one of mine does) that *aftermath* means 'the consequences or period of time following an event'. Our Smith sentence seems to fit that definition, so we are still left with the feeling that something is not quite right. But if we look at the way *aftermath* is used in a corpus, the answer leaps out. The panel overleaf shows ten examples of the way the word is used, taken from one such corpus. The negative associations are dominant. *Aftermaths* typically follow wars, fires, riots, and other unhappy incidents. So at the very least, we should amend the definition to: 'the consequences or period of time

The universe of words

Used in evidence

Ten examples of the way *aftermath* is used, taken from a corpus of written English:

...in the aftermath of the First World War...

...during the Civil War and its aftermath...

...in the aftermath of Thursday's disastrous profits announcement...

...helping to deal with the aftermath of fostering breakdowns...

...the aftermath of the fire in Bow...

...During the 1985 riots and their immediate aftermath...

...following the aftermath of the General Strike of 1926...

...In the frenzied atmosphere of the Cold War and its aftermath...

...War and its Aftermath [book title]...

...to deal with the aftermath of that tragic incident...

following a usually unpleasant event'. And that is why the Smith sentence feels odd: Smith should be happy after his election victory. To call the period an *aftermath* suggests that he had lost.

Lexicography is not just an exercise in linguistic accounting. It is a voyage of lexical exploration and discovery. Eric Partridge called one of his books *Adventuring among Words*. He was right.

Part II

The origins of words

Where do words come from? The vocabulary of a language is a salad-bowl of words of different kinds and backgrounds. Chapter 6 explores how far back in time we can go, in tracing the history of words. Can echoes of the origins of language, even, be heard in modern vocabulary? Chapters 7 and 8 examine the many sources of words in English. How many words in the language have Anglo-Saxon origins? The total is smaller than many people think. And how many foreign languages have provided words for English? The total is larger than many people think. Chapter 9 reviews the other main source of vocabulary—the strategies of word-building which allow us to make new words out of old elements. The techniques available to us have resulted in some intriguing curiosities. Part II then closes by considering an even more intriguing domain of lexical growth—the way we can use first names, surnames, and place names as origins of English words.

6 **Wordstarts**

Where do words come from? How far back in time can we go? Let's trace the history of one word, and see.

Nice. Today, it is a very general word of approval, used so often and so vaguely that many writers take steps to avoid it. In *Northanger Abbey* (chapter 14), Jane Austen has Henry Tilney say that *nice* 'is a very nice word indeed! It does for everything'. Teachers try to get their pupils to use a more discriminating word, if they describe something as 'nice'. Most of us left school with bad feelings about *nice*, as a result. (And about *get*.)

The general sense of *nice* is actually quite recent. It arrived in English at the end of the eighteenth century, and Jane Austen was one of the first to write about it. But the word with other meanings is much older. Go back 200 years more and we find its dominant senses to be 'fastidious', 'particular', or 'precise'—still heard occasionally in such phrases as *The argument makes a nice distinction*. We hear several of these uses in Shakespeare. 'Wherefore stand you on nice points?' says Richard to Edward in *Henry VI Part 3* (4.7.58).

If we go back another 200 years we find yet more senses. *Nice* first came into English with such meanings as 'foolish' and 'lascivious'. In the fourteenth century, we find one writer talking about covetousness being a 'nice sin'; another talks of someone being 'unwise and nice'. It seems it wasn't a nice word at all, in those days.

Sometime before 1300 we have to leave England, and move across the Channel. *Nice* came into English from Old French *nice*, which meant 'silly' or 'simple', and that had its origins in a Latin word, *nescius*, which meant 'ignorant'. *Nescius* came from a verb *nescire*, 'to be ignorant'. *Nescire* breaks down into two words: *ne* and *scire*—'not to know'. The word *science* comes from the same Latin word.

The origins of words

We are over 2,000 years back in history now. Written records are soon going to run out. The earliest Latin inscriptions date only from the sixth century BCE. Can we go back any further?

Scholars now know that Latin was one of the languages which evolved from a prehistoric tongue now called Indo-European. The Indo-Europeans, it is thought, were a semi-nomadic population living in the steppe region to the north of the Black Sea in the fourth millennium BCE. As they spread into Europe and north India, their speech evolved into many languages, such as Sanskrit, Greek, the Celtic languages, and Latin. By comparing the extant words in these different languages we can make guesses about the words used by the Indo-Europeans. And we find the origins of *nice* among them. It seems to have come from a root *skei-*, which expressed a cluster of related senses, such as 'cut', 'split', 'separate', 'divide'.

Common origins

Indo-European *skei-* is the origin of many words in English. An underlying sense of 'cutting' is apparent in such words as *scythe*, *scissors*, *ski* ('cleft wood'), and *shear*. And the sense of 'separating' one thing from another is there in *schism*, *skill*, *science*, *conscience*, *plebiscite*, *shield*, *shin*, the verb *shed*, and (as waste matter leaves the body) *shit*.

That is one of the wonderful things about etymology (*see* chapter 20). There are always surprises. Who would ever have thought that there was a common origin for the words *science* and *shit*?

So where did *skei-* come from? Can we go back any further than 4000 BCE? Indeed, can we go back to the very beginnings of human speech? At this point, science gives way to speculation. But it is always interesting to speculate, as long as we do not translate our creative thinking into hard fact.

We know when humans began to write—somewhere between 5,000 and 8,000 years ago. But nobody knows when humans began to speak. Anthropologists have used fossils to work out that Cro-Magnon man (who flourished around 35,000 BCE) had a skeletal structure sufficiently like that of modern humans to be able to produce a comparable range of speech sounds. These abilities would have been much less likely in the very different physique of earlier Neanderthal man (70,000–35,000 BCE). So a guess of around 50,000 years ago is not going to be too far from the truth.

One science takes us back to 4000 BCE. Another hints at 50,000 BCE. That is a huge gap. And we know nothing about what happened to language in that period. Our quest for the origins of *skei-* can go back no further. But if we examine the properties of certain clusters of words, we can speculate about what might have happened.

Perhaps, in the beginning, certain types of sound were used to express certain basic feelings or biological states, or to imitate environmental sounds. Several theories of the origins of language have been proposed which assume some such development. Primitive words might have come from imitating animal noises or natural sonic effects, such as wind and water. They might have arisen from spontaneous expressions of pain, anger, or other strong emotions. They might have been a development of the noises people make when they pull something heavy or have sex.

If something like this happened, could there be echoes remaining in languages today? Surprising as it may seem, the answer is 'maybe'. The evidence is scanty and ambiguous, but it is intriguing. It can be seen in words which seem to retain a close relationship between their sounds and properties of the real world. They are sometimes called *onomatopoeic* words (from Greek words meaning 'name-making'), but a more general label for the phenomenon is *sound symbolism*. Sounds are said to symbolize, or reflect, real-world properties.

Here is a sample of some sound symbolic words: *bubble, chuckle, dabble, freckle, nibble, sniffle, speckle, toddle, trickle, wriggle*. They all have the same structure: the words have two syllables; the second syllable is an *-l*; and the first syllable has a short vowel followed by a single consonant. They are all words conveying the notion of small size, structure, or importance, or a small movement, especially an uncertain or repeated one.

All hypotheses about sound symbolism have to be treated with suspicion. It is so easy to select just the words that suit your theory. We need to examine *all* the words in the language which have this structure, and see if they conform. Here is a larger selection which seem to fit:

> *babble, couple, cuddle, dapple, diddle, dribble, fiddle, gabble, giggle, gobble, haggle, huddle, joggle, juggle, knuckle, little, muddle, niggle, pebble, piddle, piffle, puddle, pummel, rabble, raffle, rubble, rustle, shuffle, snaffle, snuffle, snuggle, squiggle, stubble, tipple, topple, twiddle, waffle, waggle, wiggle, wobble*

But not all such words do. We might start to disagree about *bottle*, *riddle*, *saddle*, and *supple*.

We can test the hypothesis in another way, by inventing words and asking people to say what they mean. For instance, imagine a tall man and a small man. One is called *Fipple* and the other is called *Farley*. Which name goes with which man? Or, there are two alien races on a planet: one is called the *Loobers*, the other is the *Gibbles*. Which are smaller in stature? Most people give the same answers.

Another source of evidence is to look at the names given to characters in fiction, and see whether authors have instinctively supported the hypothesis. Evidence would include Jim Henson's creation the *Fraggles*, which he once called 'little guys who worked all the time'. From Charles Dickens, we could cite *Rosa Dartle* from *David Copperfield*, described as 'a slight short figure'. And if you wanted to invent a name for a race of people who go about their daily affairs without having any real idea about what is going on in the universe (at least, by contrast with wizards), then you might well choose *Muggles*.

There are more examples of sound symbolism in 'Becoming a word detective', 6. If you explore them, you will find that some will have more exceptions than others. This is only to be expected. Many of the words have been in the language a long time, and will have developed alternative meanings which have moved well away from any original sense.

Seeing the funny side

Humorists are always ready to exploit the sound symbolic potential of words. There are several *-le* place-names included in Douglas Adams and John Lloyd's *The Meaning of Liff*. They are all interpreted with reference to small or repetitive movements or things.

Beccles: The small bone buttons placed in bacon sandwiches by unemployed guerrilla dentists.

Glassel: A seaside pebble which was shiny and interesting when wet, and which is now a lump of rock, which children nevertheless insist on filling their suitcases with after the holiday.

Papple: To do what babies do to soup with their spoons.

Timble: (Of small nasty children.) To fall over very gently, look around to see who's about, and then yell blue murder.

Writtle: Of a steel ball, to settle into a hole.

And see also: Bonkle, Dipple, Feakle, Happle, Ockle, Peebles.

At the end of your investigation of English sound symbolism, of course, the exploration is by no means over. If there are echoes in English words of genuine 'original' sounds, we must expect to find them in the structure of many other languages. If they only occur in English, that tells us something about the way English has evolved, but tells us nothing about

the origins of language. So we must look at other languages, and—in theory—at all of the world's 6,000 or so languages, before we can say something sensible about the sounds which may have been used by human beings 50,000 years ago.

So, let us begin. Let us look for words for 'little-ness', which in English often have a vowel very high up in the mouth, as heard in *wee*, *teeny-weeny*, *little* ('leetle'). There it is again in French *petit*, German *winzig*, Greek *mikros*, Swahili *katiti*, Shona *ndiki*. But the word for 'little' in Welsh is *bach*. And even in English, we find *small*. It soon appears that not everyone feels the same about 'small-sounding vowels'. But of course that does not stop authors within a language exploiting the sonic potential of what is certainly there (*see* chapter 22).

7 **Wordlore**

In 1878, a Dorsetshire teacher, parson, and poet named William Barnes published a primer of Old English. He called it *An Outline of English Speech-Craft*. Why not *Grammar*? Because *grammar* is from an Old French word, *gramaire*, and to use such an 'alien' word was totally against his principles.

Barnes's aim was to promote a kind of English purified of non-Germanic words. He was particularly opposed to borrowings from French, Latin, and Greek. If he could eliminate these, he felt, English would become more accessible and intelligible—more in tune with its historical roots. English people would also become more aware of their true Germanic identity.

What made his approach so distinctive was his linguistic creativity. Not only did he use surviving Old English words in place of foreign ones, he also resuscitated long-dead Anglo-Saxonisms, and devised completely new words on Old English principles. Thus he resurrected *inwit* for *conscience*, and coined such forms as *birdlore* for *ornithology*. The coinages were often extremely ingenious, and quite attractive in their way: *forsoak* for *absorb*, *onquicken* for *accelerate*, *unfrienden* for *alienate*. *Adversative* was *thwartsome*. An *adverb* was an *under-markword*.

A tiny number of his coinages found their way into the *Oxford English Dictionary*, such as *speech-craft* and *starlore* (astronomy). But most of his lexical innovations were never taken up, and remain linguistic curiosities. It would have been surprising if it had been otherwise. It is rare indeed to find a single individual altering the character of a language's lexicon. (A famous exception can be found on p. 137.)

Barnes was by no means the first to object to the foreign words entering English. In the sixteenth century, the humanist John Cheke had felt just as strongly. In a letter to his friend Thomas Hoby, he wrote in 1561 that

(I modernize the spelling) 'our own tongue should be written clean and pure, unmixed and unmangled with borrowing of other tongues'. And in his translation of the Bible, he introduced many replacement words, such as *resurrection* by *gainrising*, *centurion* by *hundreder*, and *prophet* by *foresayer*.

Nor was Barnes the last to think in this way. George Orwell, for example, held strong views about what he perceived to be a modern trend to replace Anglo-Saxon words by classical ones. 'Bad writers', he says in his essay 'Politics and the English Language' (1946), 'are nearly always haunted by the notion that Latin and Greek words are grander than Saxon ones', and he condemns the use of such 'unnecessary' words as *expedite*, *ameliorate*, *extraneous*, and *clandestine*.

The fact of the matter, of course, is that English has grown in expressive richness as a result of its many periods of lexical borrowing. It is now possible to make distinctions of meaning that would not have been possible before. Consider the triplet of adjectives: *kingly*, *royal*, and *regal*. The first is Germanic, the second French, and the third Latin. Today we use them in all kinds of different ways. *Kingly* is for males only; *royal* and *regal* apply to both sexes. *Kingly* is used as an adjective only before a noun, whereas *royal* can be used after (as in *blood royal*). *Royal* developed a range of technical and formal uses, as in *royal blue* and *royal highness*. *Regal* developed uses to do with behaviour and appearance, as in *regal look* and *regal confidence*.

Only in humour, or for literary effect, can we break these patterns. Take *The Royal Shakespeare Company* in Stratford-upon-Avon. We can imagine a newspaper review with the headline *The Kingly Shakespeare Company*—referring to a brilliant performance by an actor in the role of Henry V. Or, if a local Stratford dignitary wanted to make an unkind point about the way the theatre was behaving, he might call it *The Regal Shakespeare Company*. Without the loan-words, such ironies would not be possible.

Doublets and triplets

There are several lexical doublets and triplets in English: alternative words of Germanic, French, and Latin origin. Here are ten of them.

Germanic	French	Latin
ask	question	interrogate
fast	firm	secure
fire	flame	conflagration
holy	sacred	consecrated
rest	remainder	residue
climb		ascend
weariness		lassitude
clothes	attire	
sorrow	distress	
wish	desire	

To lose or avoid the alternatives shown in the panel above would be to rob the language of its stylistic range. There are huge differences of resonance between them. The short Old English words contrast with the long classical words. Informal speech and writing will tend to use the former; formal speech and writing the latter. George Orwell had a point when he objected to the overuse of long words, especially when these are being used deliberately to obscure meaning. He had no point at all when he suggested that the use of such words was always a sign of bad writing. Half of Shakespeare disappears, if we eliminate the French and Latin words.

Shakespeare, of course, was well aware of the varying resonances of loan words, and it is not surprising to find several of his characters reflecting on the contrast between everyday and formal language, especially when the latter is used pompously. In *Love's Labour's Lost*, the Spanish courtier Don Armado talks of 'the posteriors of this day, which the rude multitude call the afternoon', and gets praise from the pedantic schoolteacher

Holofernes for doing so. And, in the same play, the clown Costard, having received some 'remuneration' from Don Armado, looks at the coins in his hand, and wryly reflects: 'Remuneration—O, that's the Latin word for three-farthings'.

But despite all the loan-words which have come into English (*see* chapter 8), at its core the language retains its Anglo-Saxon character. If we look not at the number of words in the language but at the frequency with which they are used, we find that all the most commonly occurring words in English have Anglo-Saxon origins. The panel opposite shows the top 100 English words, in terms of frequency. Only two of the words, *people* and *use*, are not Germanic in origin.

As we go down the frequency table, the words get steadily longer and more foreign in origin. Here are the ten words ranked 1000th to 1009th in the frequency list compiled as the British National Corpus in the late 1990s:

> *useful, extent, employment, regard, apart, present, appeal, text, parliament, cause*

There is just a hint of Germanic in this list—the suffix *-ful*. Everything else is French, and ultimately Latin.

The length of the Germanic words is their most noticeable feature. Most of them are 'four-letter words' or shorter. And it is not just because these are grammatical words, such as *the* and *of*. The words which contain some semantic 'meat' are short too:

> *say, go, get, make, see, know, time, think, come, last, give, new, way, look, use, good, find*

And if we look at the meaty Germanic words in the next fifty, the pattern continues:

> *man, want, day, thing, tell, child, put, work, become, old, part, mean, leave, life, great, woman, seem, need, feel*

Most frequent words

This is a list of the most frequent items in the 100-million word British National Corpus. The word-class (part of speech) is shown, where this is needed to distinguish different grammatical uses of the same word.

1   the
2   be
3   of
4   and
5   a
6   in (preposition, as in: *in town*)
7   to (infinitive-marker, as in: *to go*)
8   have
9   it
10   to (preposition, as in: *to town*)
11   for (preposition, as in: *for hours*)
12   I
13   that (relative pronoun, as in: *the car that I saw*)
14   you
15   he
16   on (preposition, as in: *on time*)
17   with (preposition, as in: *with ease*)
18   do (verb, as in: *I do*)
19   at (preposition, as in: *at times*)
20   by (preposition, as in: *by bus*)
21   not
22   this (determiner, as in: *this book*)
23   but
24   from (preposition, as in: *from town*)
25   they
26   his (determiner, as in: *his hat*)
27   that (determiner, as in: *that book*)
28   she

29 or
30 which (determiner, as in: *which day*)
31 as (conjunction, as in: *as we know*)
32 we
33 an
34 say (verb)
35 will (modal verb, as in: *I will go*)
36 would
37 can (modal verb, as in: *I can go*)
38 if
39 their
40 go (verb)
41 what (determiner, as in: *what time*)
42 there
43 all (determiner, as in: *all hopes*)
44 get (verb)
45 her
46 make (verb)
47 who
48 as (preposition, as in: *as a young man*)
49 out (adverb, as in: *go out*)
50 up (adverb, as in: *go up*)
51 see (verb)
52 know (verb)
53 time (noun)
54 take (verb)
55 them
56 some (determiner, as in: *some cake*)
57 could
58 so (adverb, as in: *she said so*)
59 him
60 year
61 into (preposition, as in: *into the* car)
62 its
63 then
64 think (verb)

65   my
66   come (verb)
67   than
68   more (adverb, as in: *more quickly*)
69   about (preposition, as in: *about Greece*)
70   now
71   last (adjective)
72   your
73   me
74   no (determiner, as in: *no time*)
75   other (adjective, as in: *other day*)
76   give
77   just (adverb, as in: *just gone*)
78   should
79   these (determiner, as in: *these days*)
80   people
81   also
82   well (adverb, as in: *well done*)
83   any (determiner, as in: *any questions*)
84   only
85   new (adjective)
86   very
87   when (conjunction, as in: *when we went*)
88   may (modal verb, as in: *I may go*)
89   way
90   look (verb)
91   like (preposition, as in: *like a cloud*)
92   use (verb)
93   her (pronoun, as in: *saw her*)
94   such (determiner, as in: *such larks*)
95   how (adverb, as in: *see how*)
96   because
97   when (adverb, as in: *know when*)
98   as (adverb, as in: *as good*)
99   good (adjective)
100 find (verb)

The concept of 'Anglo-Saxon four-letter words' does seem to explain a lot, but we must distance ourselves from the common usage of this phrase to mean rude words such as *shit*, *turd*, and *arse*. (The Germanic origins of *cunt* are known, and seem likely for *fuck*, but neither word is found in Old English—though hardly surprisingly, given that most of the writing was done by monks.) Catherine Cookson, in *Character* (1983), can perhaps restore a balance, and produce a genteel ending to this chapter: 'The only sort of four-letter words I use are *good*, *love*, *warm* and *kind*.'

8 **Wordloans**

English is a vacuum-cleaner of a language. It sucks words in from any language it makes contact with. Perhaps I should not anthropomorphize. A language has no life of its own. It exists only in the mouths and ears and hands and eyes and brains of its users. It is the English speakers who suck the words in. People like you and me.

English has borrowed words from over 350 languages around the world. 'Borrowing' is another misnomer. When one language 'borrows' from another, it does not give them back. 'Steals' would be more appropriate. But whatever we call the behaviour, the consequences are evident. Of the half a million or so words in English dictionaries (*see* chapter 2), the vast majority do not have a Germanic origin. Nobody has ever come up with a precise figure, but perhaps as few as 20 per cent could trace their origins back to Old English (*see* chapter 7).

I must qualify my remark: 'it does not give them back'. In the twentieth century, as English became an increasingly global language, there was a huge reverse movement in the direction of borrowing. All over the world, languages found themselves inundated with English words. Some countries even tried to stop the flow, by banning English words in public places. What they forgot is that many of the words they were trying to ban came from their languages in the first place. I remember one Frenchman objecting vociferously to *le computer*, and arguing for *l'ordinateur*. It was part of the Anglo-Saxon invasion, he said. But of course it is not. *Computer* came into English from French in the sixteenth century. It is as Anglo-Saxon as Camembert.

People tend to be suspicious of loan words, because they fear that they will carry with them all kinds of nefarious foreign cultural practices and patterns of thought. If we borrow words, we shall lose our identity, goes the argument. It is an argument without foundation. English people today do not on the whole feel any the less English because their speech uses words borrowed from French or Spanish or Hindi. There are always exceptions, such as William Barnes (*see* chapter 7), but they are just that— exceptions. If I talk about pizza, that does not make me Italian—though the fact that I have pizza available does make me appreciate more than I otherwise might what it must mean to be Italian.

It does not take long for loan words to come into a language. When something interests us, we start talking about it straight away. Within days or weeks of explorers (or tourists) arriving in a country, local words will begin to make an impact. Thomas Hariot, a servant of Sir Walter Raleigh, wrote an account of the Virginia settlement in 1588, in which he routinely uses local names (I have modernized the spelling):

> Pagatowr, a kind of grain so called by the inhabitants; the same in the West Indies is called Maize: English men call it Guinea wheat or Turkey wheat, according to the names of the countries from whence the like hath been brought.

These were the first Americanisms. Not all of the new Indian words became a permanent part of English, of course, but several dozen of them did, such as *wigwam*, *moccasin*, *squaw*, and *raccoon*. And the Web is able to show us that there are more such words in circulation today than we think. Do a search for *pagatowr* and see. One recipe page from Roanoke Island begins: 'My Mother usually makes bread from pagatowr . . .'

Loan words come from contacts between peoples. Most of the borrowings in modern English have been in the language for centuries, as a result of the first periods of contact, so we no longer have a sense of their foreign-ness. Words like *knife* and *sky* are not from Old English but Old Norse. *City* and *flower* are from French. *Desk* and *client* are from Latin. It is difficult to think of *marmalade* (Portuguese), *million* (Italian), *mattress* (Arabic), and *rhubarb* (Greek) as foreign.

On the other hand, some loans retain their foreign resonance, often because they have a different sound structure to typical English words or they are spelled distinctively. Words ending in vowels are unusual, so we notice such words as *cava*, *gnu*, *cobra*, *poncho*, and *bongo*, and may even have trouble spelling them in the plural (*see* p. 88). And one of the greatest trials facing the learner of English is how to spell the foreign words which have retained their original graphic or transliterated character: *geisha* (Japanese), *perestroika* (Russian), *bizarre* (French), *taoiseach* (Irish), *eisteddfod* (Welsh), *gymkhana* (Hindi).

A long journey

Some words have had a very long journey, with several way-stations, before they enter the English language. *Arsenic* is a good example. It is first recorded in English in 1386, borrowed from Old French *arsenic*. This derives from Latin *arsenicum*, which is in turn a borrowing of Greek *arsenikon*. But where did the Greeks get it from?

The word came into Greek from the East. If we look at Middle Persian, we find *az zarnikh* ('the gold-pigment'), which derives from the word for gold, *zar*. (Arsenic trisulphide has a lemon-yellow colour.) What seems to have happened is an example of a 'popular etymology', where people hear an unfamiliar word and reinterpret it as something familiar. This is what happens if you call *asparagus* 'sparrow-grass'.

Arsenic was used as a dye, and was reputed to have powerful medicinal properties—in particular, beneficial effects on virility. So when the Greeks heard an unfamiliar word which sounded something like 'az-a-nik', and knowing its virile associations, they naturally associated it with a word they already had, *arsenikos*, which meant 'masculine'. And the rest is history.

So is arsenic a French loan word? Yes. And a Latin loan word? Yes. And a Greek loan word? Yes. And a Persian loan word? Yes. As we shall see in chapter 20, there is never a simple answer to the question 'Where does a word come from?'

The origins of words

Loan words are entering English all the time, especially in parts of the world where the language is growing as a medium of everyday communication, such as in India, Ghana, and Singapore (see chapter 14). It is impossible to avoid them. You only have to enter a restaurant to experience the impact of fresh loan words. In a restaurant in Spain recently, I was given the 'English menu'. It contained such dishes as *Fries estrelladas and perol sausage*. I had to ask my companions to translate.

We do not think twice about most loan words, because they simply express a concept that we want to talk about. When sputnik became a reality on 4 October 1957 (p. 3), people did not stand around debating whether *sputnik* was an acceptable word or not. A new notion demands a new word, and Russian supplied it. And so it has been with *coffee* (Turkish), *caravan* (Persian), *bungalow* (Hindi), *curry* (Tamil), *soprano* (Italian), *guitar* (Spanish), and tens of thousands more.

Loan words become more contentious when they are perceived to be replacing words that already exist in the language. This has always happened in the history of English: in the early Middle Ages, Old English *milce* was replaced by French *grace*; *munuccliff* ('monk-life') by *abbey*; *boc-runen* ('book-rune') by *letter*. And it is this feeling that something is being lost by the replacement which can motivate feelings of antagonism towards loan words—as we see today when countries react against English words, and try to stop them infiltrating their languages (see chapter 7).

But the majority of a language's loan words do not replace anything. Rather, they gently elbow their way in, nudging aside already existing words and adding an extra sense or nuance to what was there before. This is the story behind such triplets as *kingly*, *royal*, and *regal* (see p. 51). Often, the new word enters because people are not entirely sure what it means, but feel it must be important if they have heard someone else use it. This was the situation which allowed thousands of French words to enter English in the Middle Ages. If the nobility were using them, it was felt, they must be important. And so they were, in the sense that, if you wanted to get anywhere in educated society, you would need to talk in an educated way—and that meant, using the latest loan words.

The lawyers were especially sensitive to these new words. The law is a profession of words, and cases succeed or fail on the basis of the way words are interpreted. So, in the Middle Ages, if words with very similar meaning were entering English from French and Latin, how were lawyers to choose the best one? The short answer is: they often didn't. They began using phrases which expressed both linguistic worlds. This is the origin of such legal expressions as *goods and chattels*—the first is an Old English word, the second is an Old French one. In *will and testament*, we have an English and a Latin word. Some of these expressions even entered the everyday language: 'Let's have some peace and quiet' (French and Latin), 'Everything's going to wrack and ruin' (English and French).

Loan words are the linguistic legacy of our ancestors. They give us an unparalleled insight into our cultural history. Some people love them; some hate them. But when we consider the way English is spreading around the world, and coming into increasing contact with other languages, one thing is certain: we ain't seen nothin' yet.

9 **Wordbuilding**

Come, go. Safari, fjord. Words like these, from Old English or abroad, make up an important part of the vocabulary of English (*see* chapters 7 and 8). But they are far outnumbered by words which look rather different:

> *happiness, sadly, unwise, nationalistic, goldfish, microchip*

These words, we feel, are composed of parts. And we can easily see the parts if we imagine them as having hyphens:

> *happi-ness, sad-ly, un-wise, nation-al-ist-ic, gold-fish, micro-chip*

It does not take long to see why such words are in the majority. For every one basic wordform, or root, we can build up several derived forms. Let us take *nation* as our root. We can add elements at the end (suffixes):

> *nation, national, nationalism, nationalize, nationalization*

We can add elements at the beginning (prefixes):

> *denationalize, antidenationalize, overnationalize*

Or we can combine *nation* with other roots, to make compound words:

> *nation-state, nationwide, nationbuilder*

And we can continue the process to include coinages which do not yet exist in the language—though, after reading them, you might wonder why not!

> *archnation, meganation, minination, protonation*
> *nationesque, nationdom, nationette, nationlet*

English is a language which allows quite lengthy sequences of elements, so much so that 'longest word' entries routinely appear in books of records. The truly longest words—chemical compounds consisting of hundreds of elements—are unprintable here. But it is possible to record the 45-letter

pneumonoultramicroscopicsilicovolcanoconiosis

recognized as the longest word in English by the National Puzzlers' League in 1935. It means 'a special form of silicosis caused by ultra-microscopic particles of siliceous volcanic dust'. Seventy years on, and we find it being used as a Web domain name. If you can be bothered to type it out, you will find yourself at a commercial website—which sells domain names!

We are fascinated by long words. Children love to play with them. They learn to mouth such forms as *antidisestablishmentarianism* before they leave primary school. But there must be some people irrationally scared of long words, otherwise we wouldn't have a word for the medical condition (which I will hyphenate, for ease of reading):

hippopoto-monstro-sesquipedalio-phobia

'a fear of long words'. Doubtless someone made it up for fun. Or maybe not.

We like to play with prefixes (e.g. *un-*) and suffixes (e.g. *-able*). Once we have learned the power of a prefix, we can use it to coin new words and achieve interesting humorous, dramatic, or literary effects. Coinages from recent years include *unban* in the 1960s, referring to the removing of a prohibition—in the case of South Africa, initially. In the 1980s we had *unbundle*, referring to the way a company can be split into parts. Then there was that interesting cluster from the middle decades of the century, including *unputdownable*, *unswitchoffable*, and *unwearoutable*. Here are some of the ones that the *Oxford English Dictionary* calls 'recent formations':

unbombed, unbugged, un-Chinese, unchoosy, un-Christmassy, uncool, unfunny, unfussed, ungay, ungimmicky, unhip, unpolicemanlike, unsorry, untouristy

*Un-*coining is not a new trend. Shakespeare has *unshout, uncurse, unsex*, and several more.

The origins of words

No matter how long a word is, it is made up using just a few basic processes of construction. That is the beauty of word creation. Once we have learned the word-building elements, we can use them to create an indefinite number of words. When we know the negative prefix *un-*, hundreds of adjectives suddenly take on a second life:

> *happy, unhappy; wise, unwise; real, unreal; complicated, uncomplicated*

Of course, the language doesn't always make it easy for us. There are exceptions and complications arising from the way English has developed over the centuries. We say *unhappy* but not *unsad*. And we say *impossible* not *unpossible*, *intolerant* not *untolerant*, and *illiberal* not *unliberal*.

How many word-building elements are there in English? Not very many in everyday use—about fifty prefixes, and somewhat fewer suffixes. Scientific language provides many more technical ones, such as *nano-* and *atto-*, *-acea* and *-ectomy*. As the panel opposite illustrates, the forms can be grouped together, on the basis of the kind of meaning they express. But again, we have to be careful. Several of the items have more than one meaning. Take *-ette*, for instance. This can mean 'female of', as in *usherette*, a 'small version of', as in *kitchenette*, or a 'substitute for', as in *leatherette*. You will need to consult a dictionary to see the range of meanings each item conveys.

Prefixes and suffixes can vary a lot between dialects, especially around the globe (*see* chapter 14). And when a dialect uses a form in a way that others do not, it often elicits surprise. Indian English, for example, uses *prepone* and *preponement* ('bringing forward') on analogy with *postpone* and *postponement*. Websites are full of comment from people complaining that they have been criticized for using this 'non-English word'. But it is a very natural and logical development, no different from *predate* and *postdate*, *prenatal* and *postnatal*, and many more such pairs. It is moreover quite a formal usage. The US Visa Application Service in India advises: 'we cannot prepone or postpone any appointments in the web appointment system'. And it has begun to appear in the wordbooks: for example, it is in the 1998 edition of the *New Oxford Dictionary of English*.

Affixing

Some common prefixes

expressing negation: *atheist, disobey, incomplete, non-smoker, unwise*

expressing reversal of direction: *defrost, disconnect, undo*

expressing disparagement: *malfunction, mislead, pseudo-intellectual*

expressing size or degree: *archduke, hyperlink, miniskirt, overflow, subnormal*

expressing orientation: *anti-clockwise, contraflow, counteract, autobiography*

expressing location or distance: *foreshore, interplay, superstructure, telephone*

expressing time or order: *ex-husband, neo-Gothic, postwar, preschool, recycle*

expressing number: *bicycle, dioxide, monorail, semicircle, multiracial*

Some common suffixes

making abstract nouns: *mileage, stardom, slavery, brotherhood, racism*

making concrete nouns: *engineer, lioness, booklet, gamester, duckling*

making adverbs: *quickly, northwards, clockwise*

making verbs: *orchestrate, deafen, beautify, modernize*

making adjectives: *republican, Chinese, loyalist, socialite*

Listen out for distinctive suffixes around the world, and you will hear them. In Ireland, you will come across -*een*, from Gaelic, in such words as *girleen* ('little girl'), *childreen*, and *spalpeen* ('scamp'). In Australia, -*eroo* gives a word a more familiar resonance, as in *crackeroo* and *sockeroo*. You will also hear familiar suffixes attached to words in ways which differ from standard British or American English. In parts of South Asia, for example, you would encounter *affectee* ('someone affected'), *freeship* ('scholarship'), and *eveninger* ('evening paper'). In parts of East Africa, you would meet *overspeeding* ('speeding'), *overdrinking* ('drinking too much'), and *oversize* ('outsize', in clothing).

There are several other ways of making words bigger. Chief among them is the combining of roots to form compound words. Most consist of just two elements. We take *earth* and *quake* and get *earthquake*. It seems a very natural process, and so it is, but we are doing some quite complex things when we create compounds. What, for instance, is the difference, linguistically, between a *hangman* and a *scarecrow*? We can gloss the first one as 'a man is hanging someone'; in grammatical terms, *man* is the subject of the verb *hang*. But we cannot gloss the second as 'a crow is scaring someone'. On the contrary: it has to be 'someone is scaring crows'; *crows* is the object of the verb *scare*. You can find a similar difference between *sunrise* and *haircut*, or between *washing machine* and *chewing gum*. All compounds contain hidden meanings of this kind.

Notice that compound words sometimes look like two separate words, because they have a space between them. Don't be fooled. If you think of their meaning you will see that they are expressing a single concept. *Chewing gum* is one thing, not two, despite the space. Often, indeed, the same compound might be spelled in three different ways, as with *racetrack*, *race-track*, and *race track*. We have seen that this causes complications when we try to count the number of words in English (*see* chapter 2).

English has some quite ingenious ways of making words bigger. One is to take a word and repeat it exactly, or introduce just a small change in its sound structure:

din-din, goody-goody, shilly-shally, helter-skelter, ping-pong

Linguists call these *reduplicated* words. Another is to take two words and weld them together to make one. So, we take *helicopter* and *airport*, and end up with *heliport*. Like this are *motel* ('motor + hotel'), *Oxbridge*

('Oxford + Cambridge'), and *smog* ('smoke + fog'), and a host of coinages that became very popular towards the end of the twentieth century, such as *sexsational* and *horsiculture*. Linguists call these *blends*. Usually it is the second element in a blend which controls the meaning of the word. So a *heliport* is a kind of airport, not a kind of helicopter.

Most unusual words?

Lewis Carroll would probably claim the accolade of 'most unusual' word creator. His 'Jabberwocky' poem, found in *Through the Looking Glass*, contains several nonsense inventions:

> 'Twas brillig, and the slithy toves
> Did gyre and gimble in the wabe . . .

Alice respectfully asks Humpty Dumpty to explain them. *Slithy*, for instance, he explains as 'lithe and slimy'. *Brillig* means 'four o'clock in the afternoon—the time when you begin broiling things for dinner'.

'You see it's like a portmanteau', he goes on, 'there are two meanings packed up in one word.' He didn't realize it, but *portmanteau word* would one day become a technical term in the science of linguistics.

Creating new words out of the parts of old ones has certainly been the most productive way of extending the vocabulary of English. It doesn't exhaust the possibilities of word creation, of course. Apart from making words bigger, we can also make them smaller, by shortening them. Some drop the last part of the word, as in *ad* (for *advertisement*) and *demo* (for *demonstration*). Some drop the first part, as in *phone* (for *telephone*) and *plane* (for *aeroplane*). Some drop the beginning and the end, as in *fridge* (for *refrigerator*) and *flu* (for *influenza*). And there are some very unusual forms, which keep bits from different parts of the word, such as *specs* (from **spec**ta**c**le**s**) and *maths* (in the UK, from **math**emati**cs**). *Turps* is a curiosity, adding an *s* to a shortened form of *turpentine*. Personal names are also often clipped in an unusual way, as we see in *Betty* (from *Elizabeth*) or *Bill* (from *William*).

This process of shortening is taken to its logical extreme in abbreviations, such as *BBC*, *DJ*, *MP*, and *USA* (*see* chapter 2). As these examples suggest, most abbreviations use the initial letters of the words they stand for—and are thus often called *initialisms*. But not all do. *TV* and *HQ* use a letter from the middle of the words. *PhD* ('doctor of philosophy') uses two letters from the first word. And many shortened words end up as pronounceable units in their own right. We say *NATO*, not *N, A, T, O*. Similarly, we say *UNESCO*, *AIDS*, and (in computing) *ROM* and *RAM*. These spoken units, whose letters are never separated by full-stops, are called *acronyms*.

There is one other important way of making new words—and that is not to change their structure at all. We just change the way they are used in a sentence. Consider this dialogue:

Child (at bedtime): Can I have another biscuit?
Mother: I'll biscuit you if you don't get off to bed right now!

Here we have *biscuit* used as a noun and then as a verb—two words, not one. We would see the differences if we followed these words elsewhere in the language. The verb would have different endings from the noun. *I've been badly biscuited*, the child might ruefully reflect, later. There are thousands of such *conversions* (as linguists call them). Nouns morph into verbs, and verbs into nouns (*It's a hit*). You can have adjectives becoming nouns (*He's a regular*), nouns becoming adjectives (*It's cotton*), prepositions becoming verbs (*to down tools*), suffixes becoming nouns (*ologies and isms*), and several other possibilities. Almost any word class (part of speech) can become any other, if you are ingenious enough.

People sometimes say they don't like conversions, but the process has a long history in English. It really came to the fore when the language lost its system of word-endings (*inflections*) at the end of the Old English period, and by Shakespeare's time it was a common technique to use words in new ways. 'My gracious uncle—', says Bolingbroke to the Duke of York in *Richard II* (2.3.86), and the Duke angrily interrupts, 'Tut, grace me no grace, nor uncle me no uncle'—two new verbs. And the pattern winds its way through later English literature. 'Petition me no petitions' turns up in Henry Fielding. 'Diamond me no diamonds' is in Tennyson. And 'But me no Buts' is the name of a 2001 punk rock group.

10 Wordnaming

'The office door was opened by the dismal boy, whose appropriate name was Blight.' Charles Dickens had a special interest in the way proper names carried linguistic resonances. Young Blight appears in *Our Mutual Friend* (chapter 8). In *David Copperfield* (chapter 44), the hero describes his housekeeper:

> Her name was Paragon. Her nature was represented to us, when we engaged her, as being feebly expressed in her name.

Authors of fiction think very carefully about the names of their characters, and often devise names which incorporate a word, or an echo of a word, that already exists in the language. No prizes for guessing which are the good guys and which the bad in this selection of Dickensian characters:

Cheeryble, Smallweed, Jingle, Gradgrind, Murdstone, Toots

It is a pattern which can be traced back to the Middle Ages. Morality plays would contain characters whose names were Goodness, Avarice, Idleness, and Ignorance. Children's intuitions are trained from an early age with such names as Prince Charming and Goldilocks. Shakespeare's creations include Belch, Dull, Feeble, Snare, and Fang. The practice continues today. J.K. Rowling's names include Bonaccord, Lovegood, Malfoy, and Voldemort.

It is a trading relationship. Authors borrow words from the language for their character names. Then, if a character becomes really well known, the language borrows them back. We can now talk of *a Romeo, a Shylock, a Fagin, a Scrooge, a Tarzan, a Lothario, an Artful Dodger, a Sherlock Holmes, a Man Friday*. Characters can become adjectives: *a Jekyll and Hyde character, a Big Brother attitude*. They can become search engines. *Ask Jeeves* derives from P.G. Wodehouse's gentleman valet. *Yahoo!* is a joking reference to a race of beings in Jonathan Swift's *Gulliver's Travels*.

When a name becomes an everyday word in a language, it is called an *eponym*. Real people are more usual sources of eponyms than fictional characters, though the relationship is obscured by the dropping of the initial capital letter. The *sandwich* comes from the Earl of Sandwich, who introduced the phenomenon during a game of cards. And there are human beings behind *biro*, *boycott*, *cardigan*, *dahlia*, *diesel*, *guillotine*, *mackintosh*, and *silhouette*, and many more objects, as well as such scientific units of measure as *baud*, *dalton*, *hertz*, and *ohm*. The names can change, in the process: *sideburns* comes from the US civil war general Ambrose *Burnside*. And they can be incorporated into a larger word, as with the *sousaphone*, from US bandmaster John Philip *Sousa*. An eponym may also recall a whole group of people: *cappuccino* comes from the colour of the habit of Capuchin monks.

It is a source of real regret to me that the proposal of the German chemist Hermann Nernst was never taken up. A great admirer of Shakespeare, he proposed that the unit of rate of liquid flow should be called the *falstaff*.

The reactions of the eponymous heroes to their lexical achievements are not usually recorded. Would the Earl of Sandwich be pleased or sorry that his name was being remembered in this way? Some names, such as *bowdlerize*, *boycott*, and *hooligan*, have negative associations. Scientists, such as Joule and Pascal, would presumably be delighted that their names live on in their professions. Mae West was also pleased when she heard that a life jacket was to be called after her: 'I've been in Who's Who and I know what's what, but it's the first time I ever made the dictionary'.

There is no sharp dividing line between common words and proper names. They feed off each other. Many medieval surnames began as common nouns, especially those associated with occupations:

Archer, Baker, Barber, Brewer, Butcher, Carpenter, Cook, Farmer, Fisher, Goldsmith, Mason, Miller, Parson, Potter, Shepherd, Smith, Taylor, Thatcher, Weaver

Some are less obvious today. *Trinder*? A wheelmaker. *Fletcher*? An arrow-maker. *Lorimer*? A spur-maker.

The origins of words

When a name is felt to be especially appropriate to a person, linguists call it an *aptronym*. We joy in the discovery that a dentist might be called Tooth. Weblists (type *aptronym* or *aptonym* into a search engine) provide wonderful examples. There is an ornithologist called Bird, a pediatrician called Babey, and a scientist specializing in animal bioacoustics called Dolphin. A famous case is Dr Russell Brain, a leading British neurologist. There was also a journal called *Brain*. It was edited for a time by Dr Henry Head. Opposites also attract. There has been a cardinal called Sin (in the Philippines) and a police chief called Lawless (in the US).

Nicknames are another illustration of the closeness of personal names to the everyday language. The origin of the word is Old English: it is 'an eke name'—an 'also' name. They vary greatly in form and meaning, but they have one thing in common: they identify people by taking their names and giving them a general character. Nor is it just people: places (*The Big Apple*—New York), sports teams (*Gunners*—Arsenal), newspapers (*The Thunderer*—*The Times*), and musical works (*Eroica*—Beethoven's third symphony) illustrate the range of entities that have been nicknamed. But people are the motivation for the vast majority of nicknames.

Near where I live, in Wales, the existence of two Dick Jones has led to one being called *Dick Taxi* and the other *Dick Ferry*, on the basis of the jobs they do. Occupation—in the broadest sense—similarly, lies behind *Jack the Ripper* and *The Boston Strangler*. Notable behaviour gave rise to *Richard the Lionheart*, *Hurricane Higgins*, and *The Merry Monarch* (Charles II). Physical description has prompted such names as *Baldy*, *Shorty*, and *Four-eyes*. Linguistic associations account for such combinations as *'Snowy' White*, *'Spud' Murphy*, and *'Dicky' Bird*. In the past decade, nicknames have received a new lease of life on the Internet, where anonymity in chatrooms is guaranteed through the adoption of a 'nick'.

'Must a name mean something?' Alice asked doubtfully. 'Of course it must', replied Humpty: 'my name means the shape I am—and a good handsome shape it is, too. With a name like yours, you might be any shape, almost.' Once again, Lewis Carroll's belligerently fragile linguistic pundit points us towards a psychological truth (in *Through the Looking-Glass*, chapter 6). We want names to mean something.

Ask any parent. The bookshops are full of books with titles that are a variant of 'Name Your Baby', and parents can spend quite some time choosing. Meaning does not always enter into the equation, of course: a name might be given simply because of family tradition: *Richard Junior* is the son of *Richard Senior*. I know a family where the father is called *Big Benny* and the son *Little Benny*. And there will be many cases where a name is chosen simply because it is fashionable (*Kylie*), or religious (*Isaac*), or just sounds nice (*Melanie*).

First-name semantics

Bernard	'brave as a bear' (Germanic)
Christopher	'bearing Christ' (Greek)
David	'friend' (Hebrew)
Eugene	'noble' (Greek)
Jamal	'handsome' (Arabic)
Kenneth	'handsome' (Gaelic)
Leon	'lion' (Latin)
Patrick	'nobleman' (Latin)
Philip	'lover of horses' (Greek)
Victor	'conqueror' (Latin)
Amanda	'lovable' (Latin)
Bridget	'high one' (Celtic)
Claire	'bright' (Latin)
Dorothy	'gift of God' (Greek)
Gwendolyn	'white, fair' (Welsh)
Hilary	'cheerful' (Latin)
Margaret	'pearl' (Greek)
Naomi	'pleasant one' (Hebrew)
Pamela	'all sweetness' (Greek)
Zoe	'life' (Greek)

The origins of words

But I also know many people who have pored over baby-name books, and been influenced by what they found there. *Felicity*, meaning 'happiness' in Latin. *Nathan*, meaning 'gift' in Hebrew. *Sophie*, from Greek 'wisdom'. *Benedict*, from Latin 'blessed'. The parents may like it—but will the child? Not everyone ends up being happy with their first name. 'It took me thirty years to work off the effects of being called Eric', says George Orwell in one of his letters.

Nor are place names exempt from influencing or being influenced by the language in which they find themselves. This is partly because there is an intimate trading relationship between the names of people and where they live. Thousands of locations are named after people, as any glance at an atlas will show. The personal element is clearly there in *Victoria*, *Georgetown*, and *Tasmania*, though obscured in such Anglo-Saxon names as *Reading* ('the place where the followers of Reada live') and *Ipswich* ('Gip's dwelling').

Place names attract attitudes too, both negative and positive, usually on the basis of how they sound. Mrs Elton, in Jane Austen's *Emma* (1816), is under no illusions: 'One has no great hopes for Birmingham, I always say there is something direful in the sound.' By contrast, Somerset Maugham's travelogue *The Gentleman in the Parlour* (1930) waxes lyrical about Mandalay: 'the falling cadence of the lovely word has gathered about itself the chiaroscuro of romance'. (*See* chapter 22, if you want to know why *Mandalay*—or *Melanie* above—is attractive.)

As with people, place names which can be interpreted as everyday words carry a real fascination. 'How did that place get its name?' is a common tourist question. And when we see some of the wonderful place names around the world, we can understand why. The US has more than most: *Difficult* (Tennessee), *Hot Coffee* (Mississippi), *Monkey's Eyebrow* (Kentucky), *What Cheer* (Iowa), *Telephone* (Texas), *Knockemstiff* (Ohio), *Boring* (Oregon), *Hell* (Michigan). You can even go on a themed travel weekend and visit *Eighty Four* (Pennsylvania), *Eighty Eight* (Kentucky), *Ninety Six* (South Caroline), and *Hundred* (West Virginia).

The story of Truth or Consequences

Hot Springs is a common name in the US—there are over thirty in California alone. In 1950, one of these places—just off Interstate-25 between El Paso and Albuquerque—had the opportunity to boost its image as a tourist centre, and took it.

To mark the tenth anniversary of the successful NBC radio quiz programme 'Truth or Consequences', its producer proposed that a US town might be willing to change its name to the name of the show. The Hot Springs Chamber of Commerce took up the idea, and in a special city election, 1,294 of the town's residents voted to change the name, with 295 against. A second vote confirmed the first, and the change went ahead. Two later votes, in 1964 and 1967, decided to keep the name—and that is what you will find when you call up the city's website today.

Everyday words can be turned into a place name as circumstances require. The exploration routes of the world are full of such names as *Cape Catastrophe*, *Skull Creek*, and *Mount Pleasant*, plus hopeful names like *Concord*, *Fame*, and *Niceville*. The same trends affect streets, parks, promenades, quaysides, markets, and all the other places where we live. Each English pub sign has a story to tell. As does each house name.

Conversely, place names can easily become everyday words. We have already seen (p. 14) how some names have developed general senses—such as the government resonance of *Whitehall*, *The White House*, *The Pentagon*, or *Number 10*. Any location can develop an independent linguistic life in this way, depending on the associations which dominate it. When a website offers a fine selection of *Hollywood* photographs, we expect film stars not streets.

The conclusion is clear. When we study words, we have to study names too, for everything influences everything. Names become words. Words become names. We look for meaning everywhere we go. And if there is

no immediately obvious everyday meaning in a name, there is someone waiting in the wings to invent one, as we have seen with *The Meaning of Liff* (p. 47).

Person names and place names are the two major domains in the field of name-study, technically called *onomastics*. But these two categories by no means exhaust the human penchant for naming. In a 1990 edition of the Radio 4 series *English Now*, over a thousand listeners sent in information to me about the things they named at home. The list included cars, computers, washing machines, house plants, wheelbarrows, and toothbrushes. I have not yet called my toothbrush Ermintrude, but I am thinking about it.

Part III

WORDS

The diversity of words

We examine the way words vary from person to person and from place to place. How do they vary, and what causes this variation? Chapter 11 examines the domain where we most readily notice—and often worry about—such variation: the spellings and punctuation marks which comprise the English writing system. Chapter 12 examines the language's sound system, in the form of the regional accents which distinguish groups within an English-speaking country and around the English-speaking world. Chapter 13 finds variation even in the grammatical endings that we attach to words. We then explore the huge range of regional, social, professional, and personal dialects and styles which forms our universe of words. Chapter 14 looks into regional dialects, nationally and internationally. Chapter 15 reviews the functions of slang, and the strong feelings people have about it. Chapter 16 probes the even more deeply held attitudes surrounding jargon. And Part III closes with a review of the most challenging and sensitive issue in the whole field of language diversity: taboo words.

11 **Wordspells**

One of the chief reasons we use a dictionary is to check on the spelling of a word. Some dictionaries even specialize in spellings: I have one on my shelves which is little more than a list of around 75,000 words. At first sight, such an enterprise seems bizarre. For how can we look a word up if we do not know how it is spelled in the first place?

But this is to misunderstand what a spelling dictionary is for. It is not for people who do not know how to spell. It is for people who *have* learned to spell, but who are uncertain about particular points in particular words. They are uncertain about how to choose between the various options the language provides. The problem with *diarrhoea* is not how it begins: it is what happens after we get to *diar-*.

There is a second reason for using a spelling dictionary. Spelling does not stand still. It changes with the times, as do other features of language, such as vocabulary and grammar. A surprising number of words in a general dictionary vary in the way they can be written: is it *moon* or *Moon*, *flowerpot* or *flower-pot*, *advertise* or *advertize*, *pediatric* or *paediatric*, *foetus* or *fetus*, *judgment* or *judgement* . . . ? Despite the best efforts of lexicographers, publishers, and printers since the end of the eighteenth century, the 'standard language' has been standardized only to a certain extent. One study found that around a *quarter* of the words in an English dictionary display alternative spellings.

We are used to seeing words in old spellings in works from the Middle Ages or from the time of Shakespeare. But even at the end of the eighteenth century, the spelling hadn't settled down. Here are some words as spelled in Dr Johnson's *Dictionary*, which was published as recently as 1755:

> *downfal, numbskul, raindeer, scissars, summersault, villany, welldone*

The diversity of words

He even formulated some rules about how he thought English was spelled. 'No word ends in -c'. Within a few years, that rule was out of date. Spelling has changed quite a bit in the past 250 years.

Why is English spelling so complicated? It is a question that has been asked since the sixteenth century, when the first studies of the subject were made by a group of scholars known as *orthoepists*. There are many languages for which a spelling dictionary is of much less value, because the relationship between sounds and letters is largely one-to-one—Welsh is an example. But such a degree of regularity has not been seen in English since Anglo-Saxon times. The present-day spelling system is the result of a process of development that has been going on for over 1,000 years. The complications we encounter now are the result of the major linguistic and social events which have taken place during this period.

The origin of the problem lies in the attempt by Christian missionaries during the sixth century BCE to crowbar the thirty-five or so distinctive sounds of Old English into their 23-letter Latin alphabet. Despite borrowing some runic letters and adding the symbol æ, it still proved necessary to use some letters (such as *c* and *g*) to represent more than one sound, and to represent some sounds by combinations of letters (such as *sc*—the equivalent of modern *sh*).

After the Norman Conquest, French scribes introduced several new spelling conventions. A number of Old English forms were replaced, such as *cw* by *qu* in such words as *quick* and *queen*. They replaced some uses of *h* by *gh* (*might*, *enough*), *c* by *ch* (*church*), and *u* by *ou* (*house*). They began to use *c* before *e* and *i* in such words as *cell* and *city*. Because the letter *u* was handwritten in a very similar way to four other letters (*v*, *i*, *n*, *m*), they tried to ease the reading task in some sequences of these letters by replacing it with *o* (*come*, *love*, *one*, *son*), thereby initiating a set of spelling exceptions. (The handwriting problem disappeared after printing became routine, but the *o* spellings stayed.) By the beginning of the fifteenth century, English spelling was a mixture of two systems—Old English and French.

Beware the 'rules'

Because of the complicated history of English spelling, few simple 'rules' ever work. There are always exceptions. For instance, most people have heard of the rule: '*i* before *e* except after *c*'. It was originally devised as a rhyming mnemonic to help people remember the difference between such words as *receive* and *deceive*, on the one hand, and *belief* and *relief*, on the other. But it had many exceptions:

- *c* is followed by *ie* in such words as *ancient, conscience, efficient, financier, glacier, science, society, species*

- *ei* can be seen after letters other than *c* in such words as *beige, deicide, eight, either, foreign, height, heir, leisure, seize, their, weigh, weird*

The only way to salvage the rule is to relate it to pronunciation. If we think of it as 'in spelling the sound "ee", then *i* goes before *e* except after *c*' it works much better—but there are still a few exceptions (such as *codeine* and *seize*).

The introduction of printing was a help, because it imposed order on the many alternative spellings found in Middle English manuscripts. A word like *might* is found in over thirty spellings during the period, and having a standard form was a great step forward in national intelligibility. But the first printers added fresh problems. Many of them came from the European mainland, and brought their own spelling norms with them. The distinctive *gh-* in such words as *ghost* is Dutch in origin.

Although spelling thereafter was much more stable, speech was not. There was a major change in the pronunciation of vowel sounds during the fifteenth century, but the spellings didn't change to reflect it. Modern spellings thus in many respects more accurately reflect the way people spoke in Chaucer's time: *name*, for instance, would have sounded something like 'nah-muh'. Similarly, because of pronunciation change, we are left with many silent letters, as in *knee* and *knight*. The *k* ceased to be sounded after the writing conventions were established.

Another kind of complication emerged in the sixteenth century, when some of the orthoepists tried to introduce a knowledge of a word's history (etymology) into its spelling. The *b* in *debt*, for example, was added by people who thought it was important to know that the word comes from *debitum* in Latin. Similarly, a *b* was added to *doubt* (from *dubitare*) and a *g* to *reign* (from *regnare*). They thought they were helping, but today we see such innovation as an extra complication. The number of irregular forms seriously increased during the period: the *gh* of *night* and *light*, for example, was extended to such words as *delight* and *tight*.

In the late sixteenth and early seventeenth centuries, a new wave of loan words arrived in English from such languages as French, Latin, Greek, Spanish, Italian, and Portuguese. They brought with them a host of alien spellings which greatly complicated the learning of longer words. Think of *bizarre*, *brusque*, *caustic*, *cocoa*, *epitome*, *gazette*, *idiosyncrasy*, and *pneumonia*. The loan-word situation continues to the present day, with such forms as *intifada*, *perestroika*, *arbitrageur*, and *chlamydia* presenting us with often unfamiliar letter sequences.

Yet another dimension was added to the spelling system in the early eighteenth century, when Noah Webster altered the spellings of many words as part of his aim to introduce an American standard. An independent nation, he felt, needed an independent system, 'in language as well as government'. On this basis, he advocated the deletion of *u* in -*our* endings (*color*) and *k* from those words ending in -*ick* (*music*), and such replacements as -*re* by -*er* (*theater*), -*ce* by -*se* (*defense*), and *ll* by single *l* before a suffix, when the stress is on the first syllable (so: **tra***veling*, but not **exce***ling*). Several of his proposals, such as the omission of silent letters (*fether*, *ile*) or final *e* (*definit*, *examin*), never caught on. But the dropping of -*k* in such words as *music* became standard everywhere.

The result is a system which is an amalgam of several traditions—chiefly Old English, French, and classical Latin/Greek. However, these are but the

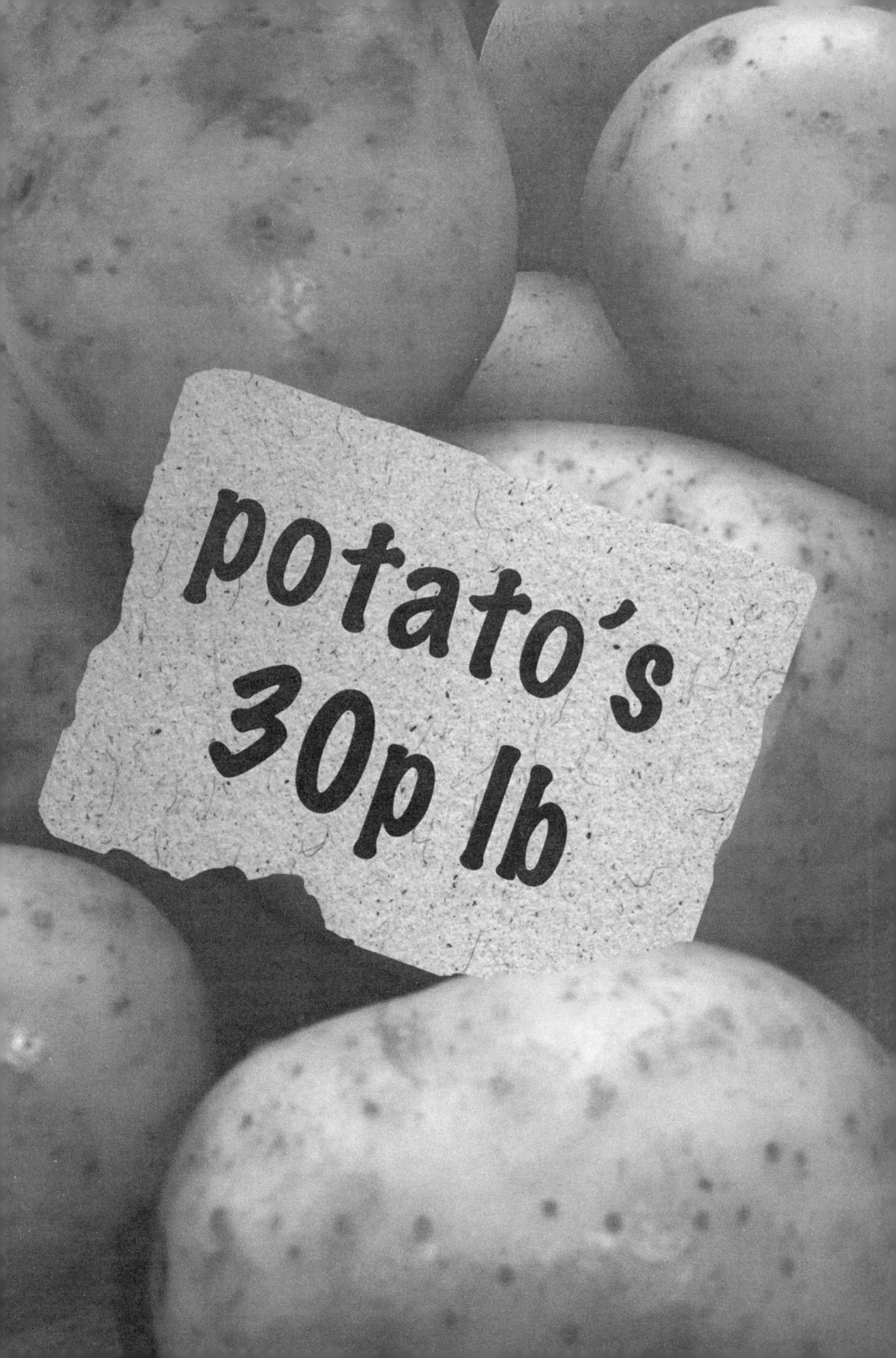
potato's
30p lb

chief sources feeding the English habit of borrowing words and their spellings from anywhere and everywhere. It is said to be one of the strengths of the language that it has such a large and varied lexicon, but this is bought at the expense of an increasingly diversified spelling system.

It is moreover a system which continues to change. During the twentieth century, American English usage increasingly influenced British, and the arrival of the Internet has been causing further changes. Accent marks, in such words as *café* and *cliché*, are usually missing on a web page, and the proliferation of websites has increased our exposure to different spelling preferences. The result has been an increase in the number of alternative forms used by educated people around the world.

Potato's?

It comes as a shock to many people to learn that a word like plural *potato's* was spelled with an apostrophe in the eighteenth century. Dr Johnson has such spellings as *grotto's* and *innuendo's*. The reason is that these words have an unusual structure in English: they end in a vowel (*see* p. 61). And writers evidently felt unhappy about simply adding an -s to make a plural, probably because the spellings like *potatos* would suggest a pronunciation rhyming with 'oss'. The apostrophe was an instinctive solution, to show that something special is happening, and it is a solution that we still use today for unusual plurals: think of *the 1940's*, *dot the i's*, and *three Bloody Mary's*, or (after a vote) *the no's have it* (few like *nos* or *noes*).

The modern system developed during the nineteenth century, when grammarians and printers tried to sort out the different ways in which the apostrophe was being used. They tried to make a sharp distinction between a noun expressing possession, which was to be marked by an apostrophe (*boy's*, *boys'*), and a noun expressing plural number, which wasn't (*boys*). This is the rule which has become part of standard English today, and the one we all try to follow.

Test yourself

Most words ending in -o preceded by a consonant came to have their plurals spelled with -*oes*. We learn this spelling rule in school— or at least try to, for there are several dozen exceptions, such as *albinos*, *pianos*, and *banjos*. It isn't easy, and few people are confident, as a result. If you don't believe me, try the following test: all you have to do is say which noun has -*oes* and which has -*os*:

> *armadillo, cargo, casino, echo, embargo, ghetto, hero, inferno, memento, mosquito, photo, proviso, solo, volcano, tomato, torpedo, veto, zero*

Look them up in a dictionary? The problem is that dictionaries do not always give the same advice. The answers given on p. 207 are those recommended by the *Oxford Dictionary of English* and *Webster's Third New International Dictionary*. Beware: some words are allowed both spellings.

So, spare a sympathetic thought for those who write *potato's*— such as the much maligned greengrocers of the land—who are intolerantly condemned to the profoundest pit by Trussian apostrophe protectionists. They are only displaying the same instinct as Dr Johnson. And there, but for the grace of a good education, go all of us.

12 **Wordsounds**

> **You say either and I say either, You say neither and I say neither.**
> **Either, either. Neither, neither. Let's call the whole thing off.**

So sang Fred Astaire and Ginger Rogers, in the film *Shall We Dance?* The words were by Ira Gershwin, and most English-speaking people are probably so familiar with them that they automatically translate the spellings into the required pronunciations. For those who don't know the song, the first line might be transliterated like this:

> You see eether and I say eyether. You say neether and I say neyether

That was the first verse. We tend to remember the beginning of the second verse too:

> You say tomayto and I say tomahto

but few of us would be able to recall all the other words which the song cites as contentious. They are actually *potato*, *vanilla*, *sasparella* (= *sarsaparilla*), *oysters*, and a cluster which have short *a* in the US and long *ah* in the UK: *pyjamas*, *laughter*, *after*, and *bananas*.

Regional differences in the pronunciations of words are called differences of *accent*, and the two most widely recognized English accents in the world are those of Britain and the US. This is because of the history of the two countries. The British Empire carried one of the accents of England around the world. By the middle of the eighteenth century it was an accent which reflected the spread of that empire—an empire 'on which the sun never sets'. In the twentieth century, an accent of the US similarly became worldwide, following the growth of American political and economic power. The British accent is usually called *Received Pronunciation*; the US one *General American*.

Although lyrics like Ira Gershwin's pack a lot into a short space, the actual number of sounds used differently between British and American English is very few. The pronunciation of *-r* after vowels, in such words as *car* and *heart*, is probably the most noticeable feature of US speech. The tip of the tongue curls back in the mouth to produce a darkly resonant sound (technically, a *retroflex* consonant). Not all Americans pronounce the *-r* (they don't in parts of New England, for example), but most do, and it has become a stereotyped feature of the 'American voice' to outsiders, satirized in such mock speech as *hrrn hrrn*.

To Americans, the most noticeable feature of British speech is the long 'ah', in such words as *ask*, *castle*, *past*, and *raspberry*. This is by no means a feature of all British speech, of course—indeed, it is just as much a distinction in the UK, separating northern and southern speakers—but it is an important sound in Received Pronunciation; and because that has long been the prestige accent in the UK, it is a sound which has travelled (along with the Empire) around the world. When Americans want to satirize Brits, they usually pick on this vowel. In *The Third Man*, the American Holly Martins (Joseph Cotton), objecting to British Major Calloway's (Trevor Howard) attitude, tells him the title of one of his books: *Death at Double X Ranch*. He then obligingly 'translates' *ranch* for Calloway's benefit: '*rahnch*'.

The pattern of emphasis in words—linguists call it the *stress* pattern—often varies between the UK and the US. Where the British say **ba**llet, Americans say bal**let**; and similarly there is a contrast between **fron**tier and fron**tier**, **ga**rage and ga**rage**, and several other words. Sometimes the contrast is in the opposite direction: UK ad**dress**, US **ad**dress; UK in**quiry**, US **in**quiry; UK ciga**rette**, US **cig**arette. The American pattern has been influencing the British, in recent decades: many younger UK speakers now say **re**search, adver**tise**ment, and **mag**azine. This upsets some British people a lot.

Other parts of the English-speaking world have their accents too. In particular, there is a distinctive group of accents in South Asia—in India, Pakistan, Sri Lanka, and Bangladesh. I say 'in particular' because of the

Transatlantic sounds

US and UK English also display a number of pronunciations affecting individual words. Here are some of them:

	UK	US
asthma	First syllable sounds like *ass*	First syllable sounds like *as*
clerk	Rhymes with *park*	Rhymes with *perk*
leisure	First syllable sounds like *le* of *led*	First syllable sounds like *lee*
lever	First syllable sounds like *lee*	First syllable sounds like *le* of *led*
lieutenant	First syllable sounds like *left*	First syllable sounds like *loo*
progress	First syllable rhymes with *doe*	First syllable rhymes with *dog*
route	Sounds like *root*	Rhymes with *pout*
tomato	Second syllable rhymes with *ma*	Second syllable rhymes with *may*

numbers involved. It is thought that a third of the population of India speak at least a basic conversational English now. That is some 350 million people—more than the English-speaking populations of Britain and the US combined. The area comprises many different accents, but some general features are noticeable, such as the 'rat-a-tat-a-tat' rhythm of South Asian speech.

From a long way away, accents in adjacent regions sound the same; but when we listen carefully, all kinds of differences can be spotted. For instance, most northern hemisphere residents would find it difficult to distinguish Australian and New Zealand accents. But differences there are. An important one is the way the two countries pronounce the vowel in words like *fish*. Australians make it more towards the front of the mouth, 'feesh'. New Zealanders make it more towards the centre of the mouth, 'fush'. Each country lampoons the other. New Zealander cartoons show Australians saying 'feesh and cheeps'. Australian cartoons have New Zealanders saying 'Sudney' (for *Sydney*).

Global accents are simply local accents writ large. The pressures behind them are the same. Accents exist to express identity, and whether the region is as large as Australia or as small as Rutland is beside the point. The communities will develop their own way of speaking, in words, grammar, and pronunciation, whatever their size. Pronunciation will be the most noticeable feature, because it affects everything that is said. You can't utter a single word without an accent.

England has a remarkable history of accent variation. A rough estimate is that, in the countryside, we encounter a noticeably different accent every twenty-five miles or so. City accents are rather different: there we can find dozens of accents packed into a very small space. There are over 350 language communities in London, for instance, and in each case the immigrant's ethnic language is combining with the local varieties of English to produce new accents. In Liverpool it is the same, but on a smaller scale. You can hear Caribbean Scouse there now, as well as Hindi Scouse, Italian Scouse, and many more.

Why is there so much variation in England? The reason is bound up with the origins of the language in the British Isles. When the first Anglo-Saxons arrived, in 449 CE, they did not come from a single part of the European mainland. According to the historian Bede, three main groups were involved—he calls them Angles, Saxons, and Jutes. As far as we can tell, the Angles came from southern Denmark; the Jutes from further north; and the Saxons from along the coast of modern Germany and the Netherlands. They would have spoken different Germanic dialects.

When they arrived in Britain, they settled in very different parts of the country. The Angles arrived along the east coast. The Saxons settled along the south coast and in the area of the Thames. The Jutes arrived in Kent and further along the south coast. So, from the very beginning, English (as it would eventually come to be called) was being spoken in different ways in widely separated regions. And as the invaders moved inland, they took their accents with them. These accent-areas would grow, and then begin to diverge as the separate communities increased in size. People north of the Thames would begin to speak differently from those south of the

The diversity of words

Thames. Any geographical barrier is going to cause accents to diverge, sooner or later. Imagine this process continuing over the course of a thousand years, and you can see why there are so many accents in England today.

Other parts of the country displayed similar variation, for similar reasons. The mountains and rivers of Wales and Scotland fostered variation there, with the additional factor that when English came to be spoken in these regions, the accents displayed the influence of Welsh and Gaelic, respectively. The contact between English and other languages is always a major factor in promoting different accents. In the new South Africa, where there are eleven official languages, English being one, the proliferation of accents is truly striking. In the old South Africa, the dominant voice was always Afrikaans-influenced. Today this is just one voice out of many. Archbishop Desmond Tutu wrote a book about post-apartheid South Africa called *The Rainbow People of God* (1994). We have to talk about a linguistic rainbow now.

Are accents dying out? That is the commonest question asked about Britain. The answer is an emphatic no. But they are changing. Some of the old rural accents are indeed disappearing, as the associated way of life goes. That is as it must be. An accent has no life apart from the community which gave rise to it. But the rural accents are being more than equalled in number by the new urban accents of Britain, fuelled as they are by ethnic diversity and by a huge increase in the mobility of the working population.

Mobility has two contradictory effects. As people move around, their accents tend to converge. We tend to speak like the people we work with and play with. And with the increase in movement to and from London, it is not surprising to see a London-tinged accent (so-called 'Estuary English') moving along the motorways and commuter railway-lines into other parts of the country, and melding with the regional accents it finds there. To a certain extent, the accents of England are becoming more similar, being influenced in varying degrees by their fashionable southern neighbour.

At the same time, mobility fosters the growth of new relationships and new communities. As we have seen in places like Liverpool, a fresh range of accents can be heard there now. Some of them, indeed, may be influenced by accents from further afield, such as Estuary English; but distinct linguistic identities are still there. And when we consider all the vowels, consonants, stress patterns, melody patterns, and tones of voice which make up an accent, it is easy to see why this is so. A combination of, say, traditional Liverpool + Estuary + Jamaican is going to end up sounding rather different from an accent deriving from traditional Liverpool + Estuary + Chinese. In *The Reader Over Your Shoulder* (1944), Robert Graves and Alan Hodge said, 'English is a vernacular of vernaculars.' It is even more so now.

A *dispute* over *dispute*

Accents never stand still. The consonants stay relatively stable, but the vowels and the stress patterns are always shifting. Some people feel uncomfortable when they notice a change taking place, thinking it a sign of the language's deterioration. But a few years later, everyone has forgotten about that particular change and is worrying about the next one. Whether we say *dispute* or *dispute* is a case in point. It is the sort of issue which today generates regular letters to the press and the BBC.

A hundred years ago, there was a similar controversy—only then it was about such words as *balcony* and *contemplate*. What could possible be controversial about them, you might be thinking? They are *balcony* and *contemplate*. Not so a century ago. Then they were *balcony* and *contemplate*. The pronunciations we take as normal now were novel then, and sources of concern.

The early decades of the twentieth century brought more anxiety, as older *illustrate* competed with new *illustrate*. That row is long since over. In the 1940s, older *promulgate* competed with new *promulgate*, as did old **controversy** with new *controversy*. The former row is over; the latter still causes occasional ripples. The current preoccupation is over words like *research* and *research*, as well as *dispute*. There will be another row in fifty years' time. It is impossible to predict what it will be; but we can be sure that, by then, the dispute over *research* will have been long forgotten.

13 **Wordendings**

Latin, German, French, and many other languages show the relationship between words in a sentence by using word endings. Linguists call them *inflections*. In Latin, for example, the sentence 'the man loves the girl' would appear like this:

homo amat puellam

The word for girl is *puella*, but the -*m* ending shows that in this sentence it is functioning as the object of the verb. If the sentence had been the other way round, 'the girl loves the man', it would have looked like this:

puella amat hominem

Now *homo* is the object, and it changes its form to make this clear.

It's a great system, and thousands of languages use it—some with just a few dozen endings, some with hundreds. If you've got inflections, it means that you can put the words in almost any order you want, and the sentence will still make sense. Once you know that *puellam* is the object, you can say

puellam homo amat
amat puellam homo
puellam amat homo

or any other combination, and the sentence still means the same thing. Word order isn't so important, in an inflected language.

Old English was an inflected language too. But towards the end of the first millennium, the inflections began to be pronounced less strongly, and they slowly died away. Once this happens, if a language is to avoid grammatical chaos, the relationships between words have to be expressed in some other way—and that means fixing the word order. In modern

English, if we want to say 'the man loves the girl' we have no choice
but to say

the man loves the girl

because if we said it the other way round it would mean something
different:

the girl loves the man

and if we used some of the other word orders, the sentence would get
very ambiguous:

the girl the man loves.

But English didn't lose all its word-endings. There are a handful of regular
patterns still in use, as the panel overleaf illustrates, plus a large number
of irregular patterns. Thousands of nouns form their plural by 'adding an -
s'. But, as every young child and foreign learner of English knows, there is
an annoying group of a few dozen irregular plurals which have to be
learned by heart. Until you learn them, you will say such things as *mouses*
and *sheeps* and *gooses*.

Adjectives also have a few irregular forms. It isn't *good – gooder –
goodest*, but *good – better – best*. They have to be learned by heart too.
But it is the verbs that display most irregularities. There are some 400
verbs in English where past time is expressed not simply by adding an *-ed*,
as in *I walk – I walked*, but by using a different ending or changing the
middle of the verb in some way. *I take – I took. She keeps – She kept.*
Again, the mistakes children or foreigners make illustrate the sort of thing
that has to be learnt: *I seed, we wented, they wonned*.

This is all part of basic English grammar. Once you've handled it, the job is
over. It would be the same if we were learning irregular verbs in French or
Spanish. You breathe a sigh of relief and move on. But there are quite a
few instance of usage in English where it is not possible to move on,
because not everyone agrees about what the endings should be.
Alternative usages co-exist. These are the interesting ones that attract the
attention of word detectives.

The common word endings of modern English

These are the regular ways of using word endings in modern English. The list does not give the many irregular forms, such as *mice* as the plural of *mouse*, or *went* as the past tense of *go*.

- We can express plural number by adding an *-s*, or some similar form: *horse – horses*.

- We can express possession by adding an *-s*, distinguished from plurals in writing by the use of an apostrophe: *girl – girl's* or *girls'*

- We can express whether a verb is singular or plural by adding an *-s*: *she walks – they walk*.

- We can express past time in a verb by adding *-ed*: *I walk – I walked*.

- We can express verb duration by adding *-ing*: *I go – I am going*.

- We can compare many adjectives by adding *-er* and *-est*: *small – smaller – smallest*.

- We can express negation by adding *n't* to certain verbs: *she has – she hasn't*.

- We can show that some pronouns are used as object in a sentence by changing their form: *I – me*.

The alternatives are not always obvious. Did you notice one in the paragraph before last? The third sentence said *learned*; the last sentence said *learnt*. To have left it like that will have brought my copy-editor out in a cold sweat! Books and periodicals generally do not allow such variation to appear, as it gives the impression of carelessness, and could be a potential source of confusion. We expect total consistency in a modern printed English text, and publishers have style books to ensure that this is achieved.

But in the language as a whole, there is no such consistency. For a host of historical reasons, many words have developed alternative forms. And this has given rise to a profitable trade in usage books, where pundits of varying linguistic aspirations and aptitudes make personal recommendations about what is right and wrong. Their judgements rarely agree.

The reason they don't agree is that they do not explore the *causes* of the variation thoroughly. Languages do not develop alternative usages for no reason at all. Languages, as I have said earlier (p. 59), do not have lives of their own. It is people who speak, write, and sign, and it is they who opt for one usage rather than another. To understand variations in usage, we must first understand variations in people, and the variations in the meanings they want to convey.

So, why do we have two forms, *learned* and *learnt*? To begin with, we have to appreciate that these are not the only words to show such variation. We also have *spelled* and *spelt*, *burned* and *burnt*, *smelled* and *smelt*, *spilled* and *spilt*, and a few more. Something is definitely up, when we see a pattern emerging like this. What could it possibly be?

Word detectives would quickly spot a difference between American and British English. We hardly ever see the *-t* verb ending in American English, other than in *dwelt* and *knelt*. By contrast, it does seem to have become more frequent in British English during the twentieth century, and also in Australia. So is there a difference in meaning between the two forms, or are they just random alternatives, as insignificant as the choice between *judgment* and *judgement*?

The detective-work needs some evidence, and that will take the form of a linguistic test. Do you feel that one of these sentences is more natural than the other?

> *The forest burned for a week.*
> *The forest burnt for a week.*

It's quite a common response to choose the first rather than the second. Why? Because the fire obviously lasted for some time, and the *-ed* ending is felt to emphasize the duration of the event more than the *-t* ending does. We are more likely to use *burnt* for an event which is sudden and short and happened once, like *I burnt the toast*. Do you agree?

There are hundreds of points of alternative usage to do with word endings in English, so investigating their causes keeps word detectives busy. They are the bread and butter of style guides. Some are very tricky to explain; some are absolutely straightforward.

The choice between alternative noun plurals is a fairly easy one. Is it *formulas* or *formulae*? *Cactuses* or *cacti*? *Referendums* or *referenda*? The regular -*s* ending is usually the more informal and colloquial. The classical ending is the more technical, learned, or formal. If I am a plant amateur, I will probably say *cactuses* when I see more than one of them. But if I am a cactus aficionado, I will almost certainly say *cacti*.

A government minister will probably talk about *referenda*. Mathematicians about *formulae*. Botanists about *fungi*. Musicians about *virtuosi*. These usages are all part of the specialist business of being ministers, scientists, botanists, and musicians. For the rest of us, we can of course use these plurals if we want to appear learned or aware. But most of the time we will simply use the regular plural, as we would any other noun.

It is a matter of stylistic choice. Nobody can dictate which style we should use. That is up to us. But we must take the consequences of our choices. If I am discussing settlements in Israel, I can talk about *kibbutzes* or *kibbutzim*. However, the implications are very different. If I use the unusual plural ending, which comes from Hebrew, I am conveying quite a level of specialist awareness. Whether that goes down well or badly with the people I'm talking to will depend on who they are. If we share a common awareness, it will be appreciated. If we do not, the usage will seem rather precious.

As always in language study, there are complications, even in the relatively straightforward world of noun plurals. Sometimes alternative plurals exist which have developed different meanings. Take *appendix*. There is a

Some word-ending variants in modern English

They've been feeding the ducks—everyday usage
They've been shooting duck—hunter's talk

The colour of the maple leaves—everyday usage
The Toronto Maple Leafs—a proper name

That cat has nine lives—everyday usage
She paints still lifes—an artistic term

Look at those little cherubs—in a creche
Look at those little cherubim—in a religious painting

They broadcast the event—preferred in UK
They broadcasted the event—preferred in US

They've mown the grass—preferred in UK
They've mowed the grass—preferred in US

They dove into the pool—only US
They dived into the pool—both UK and US

traditional difference between *appendixes* (which are found in people) and *appendices* (which are found in books). Books also have *indexes*; mathematical formulae and a great deal of technical writing have *indices*. The spirit world has *mediums*; television is one of the mass *media*.

And there are complications within complications. In American English, according to a recent survey, *appendixes* is now being used to refer to the back of a book in about 60 per cent of cases. And *indexes* is used in many cases where *indices* would be found in British English—as in *indices* of *achievement*. It is probably only a matter of time before these preferences spread into British English. It is already happening with several other forms. The other day, I heard my daughter say that one of her dogs had *gotten out of the garden*. There are over a hundred citations of *gotten* in the British National Corpus collected in the 1990s. When I mentioned this to a friend, he paused, shook his head, and said it was the beginning of the end.

It isn't, of course. In fact, *gotten* has a very respectable history in Britain. 'For he had gotten him yet no benefice', says the Clerk of Oxenford in Chaucer's *Canterbury Tales*. Rather than approaching an end, we seem to be going back to the beginning.

14 **Wordregions**

There is a story of a near-miss road/rail accident in Yorkshire. A farmer was driving his tractor towards a railway crossing. The sign said STOP WHILE LIGHTS SHOW. So he stopped, and waited until the lights began to flash. Then he began to move his tractor across the railway line. The signalman was not amused.

I'm not sure I believe the story, but linguistically it is totally plausible. For in Yorkshire English, the word *while* is often used in the sense of 'until'. *I'll not be home while midnight*. And the usage can take you aback if you're not prepared for it. I remember once being momentarily surprised when I heard a teacher say to his class: *I won't do nowt while you are quiet*.

This is Yorkshire dialect. A *dialect* is a use of language which tells other people where you are from. An *accent* tells people where you are from too (*see* chapter 12), but accents are to do with pronunciation, whereas the chief characteristics of a dialect are the way we use grammar and vocabulary. *While* is an example of a grammatical feature—a distinctive use of a conjunction. *Nowt* ('nothing') is an example of distinctive vocabulary. Most of the features which identify a dialect are to do with vocabulary. If we explored further into Yorkshire—and several websites invite you to do just that—we would soon encounter dozens of local words and phrases: *dale* ('valley'), *'appen* (= *happen* = 'maybe'), and the exclamation of surprise *eeh by gum*, which has achieved superstar status as a Yorkshire dialect marker.

We have to be careful, though, when making claims about usages being local dialect. Just because you notice a distinctive way of talking in your area doesn't mean that the usage is restricted to that area. For instance, there is one website on Yorkshire dialect which tells us that *sarnies* ('sandwiches'), *nouse* ('sense'), *jammy* '('lucky'), and *goosegog* ('gooseberry') are local Yorkshire words. They are indeed used in

The diversity of words

Yorkshire—but not only there. I used all of them when I lived in Liverpool, and I've heard them in various other parts of the country too. They are regional dialect, certainly, but not just belonging to Yorkshire. By contrast, a father's caution to his child, *You're on a Scarborough warning* ('you're in line for a punishment if you carry on behaving like that'), could hardly belong anywhere else but that county.

Everyone has a dialect, and collecting dialect words is one of the most interesting pastimes that a wordsmith can engage in. Most of the major dialects have their websites now, where people discuss local usages and add to them. In 2005, the BBC organized a hugely successful project called *Voices*, which invited radio listeners to make contributions to local dialect websites in many parts of the UK. And the Web has been a blessing to dialect freaks. If you are interested in, say, Newcastle English, typing *Geordie* into a search engine will point you towards dozens of sites. Moreover, these days broadband technology allows you easy access to some excellent audio illustrations. Then, if you are really serious, you can join a local dialect society, and become a dialectologist.

Everyone has a dialect. That claim takes some people by surprise. 'I don't speak dialect', they say. Or 'I don't have an accent.' They mean: 'I don't speak one of the regional dialects of my country.' But widen the perspective, and of course everyone speaks a dialect. British people speak the dialect called British English. To an American, everyone in Britain has a 'local dialect'. And British people have the same impression of Americans.

The global perspective is the future of English dialectology. The two big dialects of English, British and American, have long been a source of fascination for wordsmiths, but they are just the tip of an iceberg of world dialects of the language. It is an iceberg which has been growing for some 400 years, but it achieved most of its bulk in the second half of the twentieth century.

The 'new Englishes', as they are often called, followed the course of British exploration and empire-building. American English, as we have seen (p. 60), began at the end of the sixteenth century. Australian English

Dialect humour

You will often find a dialect humour book in a local bookshop. These books rely for their effect on a 'translation' from informal local pronunciation, grammar, or vocabulary into formal standard English. The joke lies partly in the spelling and partly in the very formal glosses given to highly colloquial speech.

Dialect humour is found all over the English-speaking world. A famous example from abroad is *Let Stalk Strine* (= 'let's talk Australian'), compiled in 1965 by one Afferbeck Lauder, who claimed to be Professor of Strine Studies at the University of Sinny (= 'Sydney'). In the UK, a wide range of dialects was brought together in Sam Llewellyn's helpful phrasebook, *Yacky dar, moy bewty!* (1985). Here is a small extract. A tourist has just asked the way in Scotland, and is given this reply:

Ye'll gang stracht aheid . . .	Go straight on . . .
ye'll tairn leeft fornenst the kirk . . .	turn left past the church . . .
ye'll tairn recht aneth the aik . . .	turn right under the oak . . .
and ye'll scoot through the doup o' the cleuch.	and go through the bottom of the ravine.
Mind ye dinna get lairt.	Mind you don't get bogged down.

started to develop at the end of the eighteenth century, as did Indian English. The origins of South African English date from the beginning of the nineteenth century.

But it was the independence movement of the mid-twentieth century that stimulated the growth of new international dialects of English. Think of all the former British colonies that became independent in the 1960s, such as Ghana (1960), Nigeria (1960), Kenya (1963), Zambia (1964), and Singapore (1965). New Englishes were quick to develop in these countries. Why? It is time for a thought experiment.

The diversity of words

Imagine you are in charge in Nigeria in 1960. Your country becomes independent. How will you build upon this, linguistically? English was the language of power previously. So you might well think of dispensing with that 'imperialist' language now, and using a local language to symbolize your newfound status. You look around your country and find 450 languages spoken there. Which will you choose? You quickly realize that choosing one language as the new language of power will alienate the speakers of the others. So you conclude, 'better the devil we know', and stay with English.

But then something interesting happens. Your focus on what makes your country unique leads to a fresh pride in your institutions, myths, legends, fauna, flora, music, dance, and everything else that constitutes your culture. And your attention is drawn to the words that express this local identity. All the words for local plants and animals, food and drink, clothing, tools, and crafts. Your people continue to use English, but instead of the standard British English they used before, they begin to incorporate local words and expressions into their speech and writing. The words start to appear in newspapers. They get used on radio and television. Before long, there is a new dialect, as distinctive in its own way as American English was when it first started to be differentiated from British English.

This process happened very quickly, and several times over, in different countries during the 1960s. I know because, as they say, 'I wuz there'. In 1967 Whitney Bolton and I were commissioned by a publisher to compile a 'Dictionary of English-speaking Peoples', and we set to work. We contacted all our contacts in English-speaking territories, to find out how the local dialects were doing. We were not sure what we would find, but we were bowled over by the response. There were dictionary projects underway everywhere. Lexicographers in Ghana were collecting their words. And they were doing the same in Singapore, Malaysia, India, and Nigeria. We weren't the only ones bowled over. So were the publishers. The proposed dictionary was evidently going to be much bigger than anyone had thought, and the development costs were likely to be astronomical. They dropped the project.

The diversity of words

These countries were not finding just a few dozen words. They were finding thousands. We have already seen that some regional dictionaries contain 10,000 words or more (p. 10). The scale of the exercise was already evident in the 1960s. Since then, it has grown, as more countries have achieved independence and decided to maintain a variety of English as their chief medium of communication. English is an official or semi-official language in some seventy territories of the world today.

Why are there so many local words? It isn't just to do with the distinctive identity of the countries. Local words, as we have seen in the case of Yorkshire *while* and *nowt*, can simply be equivalents of whatever exists in standard English. In Wales, children often refer to their grandmother and grandfather as *my nain* and *my taid*—Welsh words now borrowed into English. There is nothing especially cultural about this. Being a grandfather isn't a uniquely Welsh concept.

In Wales, there is just one language influencing the English spoken there. Now imagine the situation in Nigeria, where 450 languages have the opportunity to influence English. Or South Africa, where ten other official languages can influence English. It is plain that a vast number of loan words (*see* chapter 8) are going to enter the language. And if we look at one of the dictionaries of regional English, we will see a good number of them listed there. The opening page of a dictionary of South African English has *aanbod* ('offer'), *aandag* ('attention'), and *aandblom* (various flower species), reflecting origins in Afrikaans. The second page has *abadala* ('old ones'), *abafazi* ('women'), and *abelungu* ('whites'), reflecting origins in Nguni.

What will be the effect of all this regional lexical development in English? Will it mean that the language will one day fragment into mutually unintelligible varieties, as happened to Vulgar Latin over a thousand years ago? At one level, this has already happened. The kind of speech called Singlish, spoken in Singapore, is a mixture of English and Chinese, and is often incomprehensible to an English speaker lacking this linguistic background. But at another level, it isn't happening. Children in Singapore schools are taught about standard English, and the English-language newspapers they read there employ (with only minor variations) the same kind of English as would be found in London or New York or Sydney.

It's a brave new world. It seems we are all having to become increasingly multidialectal, as we travel the world. In the panel below are some extracts from news articles I read on recent travels. What do you make of them? Not a lot, unless you are into sumo wrestling, South African politics, and baseball, respectively. But increasingly, people are becoming more aware of these things. It is all part of becoming a linguistic citizen of the world.

From the English-language press

From the *Daily Yomiuri*
'Wakonahana, facing one of the few rikishi smaller than himself, had little trouble with No. 6 maegashire Mainoumi, who could use none of his tricks against the technically-sound sekiwake.'

From the *Sunday Times* (South Africa)
'It is interesting to recall that some verkrampte Nationalists, who pose now as super Afrikaners, were once bittereinder bloedsappe.'

From a US Web report
'Brown was hit in the helmet by a Jim Taylor pitch in the top of the eighth inning and was down at home plate for three minutes.'

Glossary (for UKcentric users)

rikishi: 'strong man' – a professional sumo wrestler

maegashire, sekiwake: rankings in the sumo divisions

verkrampte: bigoted

Afrikaners: Afrikaans-speaking white South Africans

bittereinder: die-hard

> *bloedsappe*: staunch members of the United Party
>
> *pitch*: the act of pitching or serving the ball to the batter
>
> *inning*: innings
>
> *home plate*: the area at the apex of the diamond where the batter stands, and which must be touched by the base runner before a run is scored

So, where are you from, linguistically? Somebody might answer: Stepney, the East End, London, England, Great Britain, the UK . . . All answers are correct. And each answer has a linguistic counterpart in the form of a dialect. In some cases, we can go more widely than an individual country. South Asian English includes all the countries that make up the subcontinent of India. In other cases we can locate people even more narrowly. Shaw's Professor Henry Higgins (in *Pygmalion*) claimed: 'I can place any man within six miles. I can place him within two miles in London. Sometimes within two streets.' He was exaggerating a bit. But only a bit.

15 **Wordgangs**

The chief use of slang
Is to show that you're one of the gang.

I can't remember where I first learned this jingle, but it has stayed with me. It summarizes in a few words the essential point about slang—that it identifies a social group which is very conscious of its identity. We usually associate slang with the street, with young people, with the latest fashions. But this is to miss a general point. For we all use slang. We all belong to gangs.

Here are some of the gangs I've been part of this past week. One day I was a member of a linguistics gang, and swopped gossip about syntax (yes, that is possible) using informal jargon that would have been unintelligible to outsiders. Another day I found myself working with a theatre gang, and encountering a quite different lexical world, full of actors *drying* ('forgetting lines'), *notes* ('director's comments on performance'), and *get-outs* ('moving scenery onto transport after a show'). A third day found me in a business gang, where all the talk was of *leveraging assets* and *exit strategies*. And at random moments I talked to my gang of children, whose ages span the best part of fifteen years, and who reflect in their speech their individual periods of linguistic gestation. The oldest one doesn't say *wicked* (= 'good'); the youngest one does.

Everyone belongs to multiple gangs. And the membership of the gangs reflects a wide range of variables. Some gangs are based on age. Indeed, these are probably the most noticeable kind. The vocabulary of senior citizens is a world apart from that of their grandchildren. But the gap need not be so great. The vocabulary of year 10, in school, is often different from that of year 9. A few months of age, when you are young, can make a great deal of linguistic difference. 'If I said *phat* ['great, really cool'], my mates would just laugh at me', said one fifteen-year-old. But a year lower down in his school, everyone was saying it.

As we look back at earlier ages, we can see the lexical worlds of long-dead gangs. In 1712, Jonathan Swift, in an essay on improving the English language, complained bitterly about the bad habits of university students who

> come up to town, reckon all their errors for accomplishments, borrow the newest set of words, and if they take a pen in their hands, all the odd words they have picked up in a coffee-house, or a gaming ordinary, are produced as flowers of style.

He was thinking, amongst other things, of abbreviations such as *pozz* ('positively'), *phiz* ('physiognomy'), *rep* ('reputation'), *mob* (Latin 'mobile', pronounced 'moh-bi-lay'), and *incog* ('incognito'). *Mob*, of course, has since become standard English.

Slang, by its nature, tends not to be used for long. Either it is picked up by the rest of society, becoming part of general usage (as in the case of *mob*), or it goes out of fashion and is eventually used by no one. The pages of Eric Partridge's *Dictionary of Slang and Unconventional English* are full of such long-dead expressions—and we need a dictionary in order to interpret them. What are *hoosh*, *mocteroof*, and *prosser*? (Some of Partridge's explanations are shown in the panel opposite.)

Actually, I say they are long dead, but who knows if these words are not still lurking in someone's usage somewhere, even after centuries? It is never possible to be absolutely definite about the currency of words which have their existence chiefly in speech (as opposed to writing). We can often tell when slang is new, current, or dated, but it is difficult to generalize. Take these phrases, used by a teenager at one end of a mobile-phone conversation, overheard on a train in 2005:

Hey, man, wassup?	*Awesome.*	*No way!*
That, like, rocks.	*Way rad.*	*That so sucks.*
Majorly.	*Yeah, right.*	*Whatever.*
See you later, dude.		

Slanguage

Examples of (probably) dead slang:

hoosh: a thick soup with plenty of body (1905)

mocteroof: to doctor damaged fruit or vegetables (Covent Garden, 1860)

prosser: a cadger of refreshment (c.1880)

And some others:

crusty-gripes: a grumbler (1887)

whiffled: tipsy (c.1930)

giggle-water: champagne (c.1910)

truck-gutted: pot-bellied (1860)

buy the rabbit: to have the worst of a bargain (1825)

Several of these are signs of the times. *Whatever*, for instance, meaning 'We don't need to talk about this further'; *See you later*, in the sense of 'I will talk to you again another time' (not necessarily today, and not necessarily a visual meeting). These have become fashionable over the past couple of years. But the last word in this list surprised me. I had thought *dude* had gone the way of all flesh, along with *most totally excellent*, and all the other phrases popularized by films starring Bill and Ted (Keanu Reeves and Alex Winter) in the late 1980s. Apparently not.

The problem with slang is that individual cases do not make a generalization. If a group of teenagers say they never use a word, that tells us nothing about its status. It may be a personal dislike, or something local to a particular class, or school, or town, or area. The word may not even have reached that area yet. We have to listen to a lot of people over a wide area before we can be sure of a trend. And sometimes, if we are in the right place at the right time, we can spot a trend being born. I had this experience a few years ago.

The diversity of words

In 2003 I found myself watching the Channel 4 reality TV show *The Salon*—set in a hairdressing salon, with staff and customers filmed all day, tantrums and all. You might think this odd behaviour for an academic linguist, but there were reasons.[1] And, in the event, I learned a lot, linguistically. When people get their hair done, there comes a point when the hairdresser asks them whether they like the result. Most people say they do, using a conventional expression. I would say *That's fine, thanks*, or *Very nice*. Not so among *The Salon's* clientele. Some of them would say *Cool* or *Wicked*. That I was expecting. But I wasn't expecting to hear *Evil*, *Brutal*, and a number of other negative words which were evidently then being used as expressions of delight in London. Checking my files later, I realized I had heard one of these before—*brutal*, used in exactly this way in Ghana, in the 1980s. But I had never heard it in the UK before.

A few days after I heard these usages I found myself in Southampton, talking to a group of A-level students. We talked about slang, and I asked them what they would say in these circumstances. They admitted to *cool* and *wicked*. But they had never heard the others. However, a year later, back in the same school and talking to another A-level group, the situation had changed. *Brutal* was now a familiar usage. Indeed, why was I even bothering to ask? Doesn't everyone use it? (I often wonder whether my illustration of it the year before had been a facilitating factor. Now that would have been a first. And I can imagine the headlines: PROF TEACHES SCHOOLKIDS TO SPEAK SLANG. Read all about it.)

Age is a very important factor involved in the evolution of slang, but it is by no means the only one. Gender is important too. Boys and girls will each have their preferences, and immediately sense when an expression belongs to one group or the other. Ethnic variation is a huge driving force, especially in an increasingly multicultural society. Occupation can be a factor, as in Cockney rhyming slang, originally thought to have developed as an argot within the criminal profession (*plates of meat* = 'feet'; *apples and pears* = 'stairs'). Educational background is highly relevant: all schools

---

1 My actor son Ben was 'the voiceover man'.

have their own slang, with some of the oldest schools having especially elaborate traditions. And the social class a person belongs to—however this is defined—has its linguistic consequences in the form of class-identifying slang. *What-ho, old bean? Feeling a bit squiffy? You are a chump.*

Those examples are from the 1920s—*squiffy* is 'tipsy'—and there is a lot more in the Wooster and Jeeves dialogues of P.G. Wodehouse. We can find analogous examples in any decade, of course, and related to any social class we wished to recognize. Or to any occupation. For the jobs we do are one of the most important ways in which our individual wordhoard grows and the vocabulary of the language expands (*see* chapter 16).

People do get unnecessarily worried about slang. They continue to associate it with 'persons of a low or disreputable character' (as the *Oxford English Dictionary* describes the word's original use in the eighteenth century). They think it is somehow causing the language to deteriorate. Some of our best authors think otherwise. In a famous essay in defence of slang (1901), G.K. Chesterton wrote: 'All slang is metaphor, and all metaphor is poetry'. John Galsworthy, in *Castles in Spain* (1927), comments on the fundamental place of slang in fostering a language: 'Slang is vigorous and apt. Probably most of our vital words were once slang'. And Carl Sandburg famously defended it in a letter to the *New York Times* in 1959: 'Slang', he wrote, 'is a language that rolls up its sleeves, spits on its hands and goes to work.'

The metaphors continue throughout literature—slang as life-blood, a sport, or a fermentation. Eric Partridge, who studied it more than most, called it 'the acme and quintessence of spoken and informal language'. Certainly I cannot think of another area of vocabulary which conveys more insight into how we live and think. It plays a major role in explaining the diversity of English. But we must not exaggerate its significance. It is not the whole story of the lexicon, by any means. In fact, if quantity is the criterion, there is another area which is much more important, because it contains far more words than slang, and that is the jargon of the professions.

The rise and fall of slang

A slang word can rise and fall within a decade. *Bling bling* arrived in English in the late 1990s, used to describe diamonds, jewellery, and all kinds of showy clothing accoutrements. It became nationally known in the US when Cash Money artist BG (Baby Gangsta) made a hit hip-hop song called 'Bling bling', and it soon arrived in Britain, where it was more usually used without the reduplication: *bling*. It appeared in the fifth edition of the *Shorter Oxford English Dictionary* in 2002, and in the fourth edition of the *Longman Dictionary of Contemporary English* in 2003—the latter aimed at foreign learners of English. It had arrived.

The sound symbolic character of the word (*see* chapter 6), redolent of the glistening light reflected by metal, caught popular attention. *The Times* ran an article on it. There is now a gold teeth specialist in Las Vegas called Mr Bling. It is the title of a novel by Erica Kennedy (2004). And the same year it was the name given to a thrill ride at Blackpool Pleasure Beach. Its sense began to broaden, as people began to use the word in new ways. The website ThinkBling defines it as 'anything shiny and worth a good amount of money'. Cars can now be bling. Even that definition is passé. A rich meal can be bling. 'Bling breakfast' was the headline of a newspaper article in New York in 2004.

But the word's takeover by the middle classes has made it worthless to the rapping community. My rapping contacts tell me they would never use it now (late 2005), except as a joke. Whether it stays in popular usage in the non-hip-hopping world remains to be seen.

16 **Wordworlds**

There is no language-related word that the public hates more than
***jargon*—unless it is *cliché* (*see* chapter 19). But jargon holds a**
special place in our minds because there is so much of it. And it hits
us, often, when we are least able to handle it—when we are
unwell, or in trouble, or trying to fill in a tax return. The
vocabulary (and grammar) of medicine, law, and civil bureaucracy
is often, to the average person, a barrier to understanding. And
when this happens, we feel, rightly, that something has gone
seriously wrong. That is not how language is supposed to work.

What causes jargon? We have to make a distinction straight away.
Doctors understand medical vocabulary. Lawyers understand legal
vocabulary. Civil servants understand bureaucratic vocabulary. So there is
nothing intrinsically wrong with the meanings of the words themselves.
The problem must lie in the way they are being presented to us. Words
aren't harmful. They are, after all, only mouthfuls of air, handfuls of marks
on a surface, or clusters of pixels on a screen. It is the people who control
the mouths, hands, and screens that are the problem.

If I said to some phonetician colleagues, 'Lucy's voiceless sibilant
articulations are being replaced by voiceless interdental fricatives in
syllable-initial positions', I would expect them to understand me, and I
wouldn't expect any criticism for my use of technical terms. It is a perfectly
clear statement—to them. But if, after a speech therapy session at a clinic,
I met Lucy's mother, and offered her the same sentence, I would expect
both incomprehension and criticism. What my sentence means, turned
into everyday speech, is 'Joan's got a lisp at the beginning of her words'.
And that is what I would have to say to get my message across. I have to
translate. It's my problem. Not Lucy's mother's.

All specialists are in the same boat, when it comes to communicating with
the public. And if they had all taken the trouble to remember the gap

between their knowledge and the knowledge-level of their audience, the issue of jargon would never have arisen. But that, it seems, is not the human way. We encounter jargon in every walk of life, in hire-purchase documents and insurance forms, in contracts and licences, in medicine labels and safety instructions, and in many other contexts where we find our rights and responsibilities defined. So either people are not capable of bearing their audience in mind when they speak and write, or they do not want to bear their audience in mind. Which is it? Cock-up or conspiracy?

There are supporters of both views, and there is evidence in support of both views. Those speakers and writers who belong to the first camp are usually ready to do something about it, when the problem is drawn to their attention. Those belonging to the second camp become defensive and evasive, and do not do anything about it (though they may claim they do).

These days, most bodies which deal with the general public are prepared to rework their material, once they appreciate that there is a serious problem. But obviously, the problem has first to be drawn to their attention. This is where organizations like the UK's Plain English Campaign come in. They were adept at first bringing the issue of gobbledegook into the public arena. In 1979 the Campaign was launched by a ritual shredding of government forms in Parliament Square in London. The act seemed to touch a nerve. The effect was immediate. By 1985 over 21,000 forms had been revised, and a further 15,000 withdrawn.

The same thing happened in the US. In 1978, President Carter issued an order requiring that regulations be written in plain English. The act promoted a great deal of local legislation throughout the country, and an increase in plain language awareness among corporations and consumers. US policy has vacillated since, but the benefits of the campaign have been felt everywhere. Companies made huge savings in time and money as a result of using clearer language. Less time was needed to deal with queries, or in having to return badly completed forms because the instructions were unclear. The Plain English Campaign has estimated that sloppy letter-writing alone costs the UK about £6,000 million a year.

The (other) Crystal mark

In 1990, the Plain English Campaign introduced a seal of approval to encourage organizations to communicate clearly with the public. They called it the Crystal Mark. I don't think they had the present author in mind when they named it.

Here are the criteria, if you want your documents to achieve this accolade (I quote from their website):

- a good average sentence length (about 15 to 20 words);

- plenty of 'active' verbs (instead of 'passive' ones);

- everyday English;

- words like *we* and *you* instead of *the insured, the applicant, the society,* and so on;

- conciseness;

- clear, helpful headings with consistent and suitable ways of making them stand out from the text;

- a good typesize and clear typeface;

- a reasonably short average line length; and

- plenty of answer space and a logical flow (on forms).

In both countries, the campaigns continue. In the UK there are the annual Plain English awards, applauding good practice and vilifying bad. The Golden Bull award is given to the worst examples of gobbledegook. Here is one 'winner' from 2004. It is an extract from an email to a customer from a telecom organization.

> BT have started processing the first stage of our MPF orders i.e. the line test and production of a line characteristics report. However with the second stage (i.e. physically installing the metallic facility path

between the customers line and the Trilogy equipment) they will only walk one or two orders through the system Thursday of next week.

Physically installing the metallic facility path? Laying the cable.

In the US the Doublespeak Awards, sponsored by the National Council of Teachers of English, do a similar job. The award is given to a public figure who uses language that is grossly deceptive, evasive, euphemistic, confusing, or self-contradictory. In 2003 it was awarded to George W. Bush, for his statements regarding the reasons why the United States needed to pursue war against Iraq.

These two examples illustrate the two views mentioned above. The telecom example is an example of ineptness. There is, one imagines, no deep plot within the company to confuse the client. Only the most paranoid of customers would think so. By contrast—and without this book needing to take sides in the matter—it is a matter of common observation that an awful lot of people are deeply unhappy about the Iraq situation, and attribute a policy of deliberate obfuscation behind US government statements.

Politicians always get the most flak. A Doublespeak Award could be given to virtually any politician in any country at any time. Fortunately, ordinary members of the public are aided by a country's journalists, consumer groups, watchdog committees, and comedians, who keep an eye on political language and bring it down to earth whenever they can.

Gobbledegook awards are a good thing, in the way they keep the problem of unclear language in front of everyone's minds. They are not without their problems, though. They can fail to distinguish between difficulty and clarity, and often do not take audience into account. A text can be difficult and yet clear. Here is a sentence from a university report on a new corporate design:

> The geometric foundation of the design is based upon a circular form, which makes reference to the Institution's global perspective and international reputation in teaching and research.

Being evasive

Being evasive is not just something politicians do. It affects us all. Here is a selection of expressions used over the past decade by 'ordinary employers' in press announcements about cutting back on their workforce:

- chemistry change
- dehiring
- deselection
- destaffing
- downsizing
- executive culling
- involuntary separation
- negotiated departure
- personnel surplus reduction
- reducing headcount
- rightsizing
- skill-mix adjustment

Sometimes evasive terminology is there for the best of reasons. Not all people in power are hard and unfeeling; many try to soften the blow of bad news, and use language which is sympathetic and face-saving. But few would sympathize with the motivation which led to some of the above expressions.

The desire to save pain can lead to some bizarre recommendations. In 2005 there was a proposal in the UK that the term *failure* should not be used in schools, but should instead be replaced by *deferred success*. Howls of derision followed.

But the moral is plain. While condemning unnecessary or obscuring language in others, we should not forget to look out for it in ourselves.

The diversity of words

You have to concentrate, but the text is, to my mind, perfectly clear. And 'my mind' is what counts, as I am a typical member of the audience to which this statement was being addressed. This is not gobbledegook. Nonetheless, the report got a Golden Bull in 2001.

Plain English involves more than just vocabulary, of course. It involves grammar—avoiding long and complex sentences—and layout. The way text is presented on a page can be just as important as its linguistic content. But at the end of the day, vocabulary is king. No matter how easy a sentence is, and how clear the layout, if we don't understand the words it contains then we will not be able to understand it.

But now this chapter changes tack. Whose responsibility is it to understand vocabulary? Is it entirely the producer's? Communication is a two-way enterprise, a shared responsibility. If I go to Norway, speaking no Norwegian, and someone speaks to me in that language, would I be right to complain, and say it's their problem that I didn't understand? That would be absurd. It is my responsibility to learn enough Norwegian vocabulary to survive.

It is the same with our mother tongue. Education is the process of preparing us for the big world, and the big world uses big words. The more big words I know, the better I will survive in it. Because there are hundreds of thousands of big words in English (*see* chapter 2), I cannot learn them all. But this doesn't mean that I shouldn't try to learn some.

In fact, of course, we do learn some. Everyone has acquired some technical terms for some areas of living. And I mean everyone. They might be terms for parts of motorbikes, or positions and moves in football, or garden plants, or the situations in computer fantasy games, or the magical world of Harry Potter, but they are terms nonetheless. I know a ten-year-old who can talk at length about dinosaurs, using vocabulary that is well beyond me. And most adults express appalled admiration at the impenetrable nature of teenage text-messaging.

Ear, Nose and Throat Department

The diversity of words

To call all this gobbledegook is to miss the point. There is a need for technical terms in everyday life, and the more we can extend our knowledge of specialist nomenclature, the more we will get more out of everyday life. We can't all be lawyers, or doctors, or scientists. But we will all gain from learning something about the vocabulary of law, of medicine, of science. And that is one of the things that popular books of science and many word-books try to do. The *v* of vocabulary could just as well stand for 'value-added'.

There are limits, in both directions, in relation to the professions. There is a limit to how much legal, medical, or scientific vocabulary we can learn, but there is also a limit to how much simplification the specialists can introduce. The language of the law, in particular, is complex because the thinking it is trying to convey is complex. When we are dealing with a domain where a case stands or falls on a particular choice of words, or even punctuation, and where earlier uses of language have to be closely compared with a present-day one, it is easy to see why lawyers have a complicated linguistic game to play. Everyday language is very prone to ambiguity. Legal formulations are precise. The public needs to have confidence in legal formulations, and such confidence can come only from lawyers using language that has been tried and tested in the courts over many years.

It is a tricky balancing act. We need to do our bit, and the specialists need to do theirs. It is no defence to say: our field is complex, therefore we do nothing. Rather, all professions need to say: our field is complex, so let us explore ways of expressing its subject-matter more clearly when addressing the general public. The principle is gradually being accepted, even in the legal profession. In 1990 the Law Society in Britain published a drafting manual. It was called 'Clarity for Lawyers'.

17 **Wordrisks**

Words, like guns, can be loaded. And, like guns, they can threaten, hurt, and wound. They can even kill—relationships and reputations. There are always risks, when we use words. And it makes sense to try to understand what these risks are. We use words so naturally, but that does not mean we should use them lightly.

A US writer on semantics, S.I. Hayakawa, once distinguished between 'snarl' words and 'purr' words. *You filthy scum*, he suggested, is little more than a verbal snarl, whereas *You're the sweetest girl in the world* is the linguistic equivalent of a feline purr. It is surprising how many words in the language snarl and purr.

They sometimes turn up in magazine competitions. Readers would be asked to find 'irregular verbs' which work in this way:

I am firm
You are obstinate
He/she is pig-headed

One such competition, in the *New Statesman*, elicited such entries as:

I am sparkling
You are unusually talkative
He is drunk

I day dream
You are an escapist
She ought to see a psychiatrist

There are many such nuanced three-word groups in English: *slender – thin – skinny*; *frank – blunt – insolent*; *overweight – plump – fat* . . .

The diversity of words

Whatever the intentions of the user, the choice of words will have an immediate effect on the listener. And faced with tears or anger, it's not much use saying 'But I didn't mean . . . '. If we use a word, our listeners naturally assume we have used it intentionally. That is how conversation works.

So we have to anticipate the nuances of words, and develop our ability to be in conscious control of them. If we want to purr, then we need to know which words will best convey that mood. And if we want to snarl, likewise. It's up to us which we do. Being pleasant or unpleasant is a matter of psychology, not linguistics. But it isn't always obvious which words will do the right job, because of language diversity and change. What is a purr word to me might be a snarl word to you. And what was a purr word yesterday might be a snarl word today.

The phenomenon of political correctness (PC) is a perfect illustration. Some of the most loaded words in the language are to do with the way society talks about itself, and especially about groups of people perceived to be disadvantaged or oppressed. The most sensitive domains are to do with race, gender, sexual affinity, ecology, and (physical or mental) personal development. Hundreds of words are involved.

During the 1980s, an increasing number of people became concerned to eradicate what they saw to be prejudice in these areas, and focused on vocabulary in order to do so. The thought was that, if demeaning words could be eliminated, social improvement would automatically follow. It was a naive expectation. The PC movement certainly made everyone aware of the fact that there was an issue that urgently needed solution, and that language was a part of it. But the suggestion that by eradicating offensive language we would eradicate social attitudes and inequalities betrayed a lack of understanding of how language works.

What has been happening is a very natural language process. The replacement of one word by another has not led to the snarl connotations of the first word disappearing. In the absence of corresponding changes in social attitudes, they simply transfer to the replacement word. A proposal in the 1990s to replace *mental handicap* by such phrases as *learning difficulties* or *intellectually challenged* did not help. As the marketing director of the British charity Mencap said at the time: 'It is only a matter of time before even the most right-on expression becomes a term of abuse. Children are already calling each other LDs as an insult.'

It was the same with *disabled* and *differently abled*, *Third World* and *developing nations*, *negro*, *black*, and *African American*. And there was a further complication. Who was to decide whether a word was snarl or purr? *Black* is a famous case. When this word was condemned in the 1980s as demeaning to African Americans, there was a campaign which left people scared of using the word, even in unrelated everyday vocabulary such as *blackboards* or the *black* pieces in chess. But in a 1991 survey in the US, over 70 per cent of blacks said they preferred to be called *black*.

There is a big difference, also, between written and spoken English, when it comes to implementing PC guidelines. It is possible for any of us to look at what we have written and decide whether it is contentious in any way, and then change it. But it is not possible to monitor our spontaneous speech efficiently. It is only a matter of courtesy and common sense to try to avoid words which our audience would find insulting—unless, of course, it is our intention to insult them. But it is impossible to eliminate the idiomatic habits of a lifetime—something that was especially apparent when there was feminist criticism of such idioms as *Tom, Dick, and Harry* or *the man in the street*. It takes time for language habits to change.

PC proponents want change yesterday. Social change can indeed be introduced overnight, for example by a parliamentary act. But linguistic change cannot. It is impossible to legislate for language. The failure to understand this basic linguistic point lies behind the mounting criticism of hardline PC campaigners as being 'language police'. The blanket condemnation of people for using certain words has been described (in an *Economist* editorial) as 'the most pernicious form of intolerance'. It would be a great shame if the original highly laudable motivation for the movement were to be obscured by its excesses; but that seems to have been the case. The term *PC* has itself become a snarl word.

Taboo vocabulary sometimes falls under the heading of snarling, but not always. In a language context, the term *taboo* refers to words which people avoid using, because they believe them to be harmful, embarrassing, or offensive.

- *Harmful?* If you are superstitious, or hold certain religious beliefs, you might well avoid certain words, believing that they will do you no good. Naming the devil, for example, or saying *Blimey* (= 'God blind me'). We are all suspicious about some names, even if we don't really believe we are superstitious. Which of us would call our new boat *Titanic*?

- *Embarrassing?* Some people avoid colloquial words to do with the sexual organs and the sexual act, such as *cock* and *fuck*. Some do not refer directly to dangerous diseases and death; they talk about *falling asleep* ('dying') and *caskets* ('coffins'). It is difficult to determine embarrassment levels, as these are more to do with people's personalities than with words. Fictional role-model Bridget Jones and her readership are evidently unembarrassed by *shagging*. Comedian Jasper Carrott and his viewers seem unconcerned about *bonking*. But I know people who would go bright red if they heard either of these words.

- *Offensive?* It can be uncomfortable talking about the various substances exuded by the body, and many people do not like using such words as *shit*, *piss*, and *pee*. The only alternative is to find an indirect expression which everyone understands —a euphemism— such as *take a leak*, *spend a penny*, *visit the little boys'/girls' room*. Under the heading of offensive we also need to include the various forms of physical, mental, and social abnormality which are the focus of political correctness.

The definition of taboo has an interesting consequence. If certain words are not felt to be harmful, embarrassing, or offensive, then they cannot be taboo to the speakers. And of course we encounter this all the time. It all depends on the setting, and on who the speakers are, and what their relationship is to each other. The other day I heard two young men laughing together in the street, and one called the other a *fucking cunt* in response to some joke. To many people, this is maximally offensive language. To them, it was evidently a term of endearment.

A bloody history

On 28 May 1714, Jonathan Swift commented, in one of his letters to Stella, that 'it was bloody hot walking today'.

Almost exactly 200 years later, on 11 April 1914, the *Daily Sketch* carried the following headline:

> TO-NIGHT'S 'PYGMALION', IN WHICH MRS. PATRICK CAMPBELL IS
> EXPECTED TO CAUSE THE GREATEST THEATRICAL SENSATION FOR YEARS

> She was going to say 'Not bloody likely'—a word, which the *Sketch* commented, 'is certainly not used in decent society'.

But the pendulum swings. Seventy-five years on, and we find Prince Charles saying that English 'is taught so bloody badly' these days.

Passers-by can be horrified at the 'language' of young people these days. What they are doing is imposing their own sensibilities about taboo onto the speakers, and assuming that the words mean the same thing to the youngsters as they do to them. But this isn't so. The words may be the same, but their functions are different. Swearing among young people is as much a matter of maintaining rapport as giving offence. It is gang-building behaviour (*see* chapter 15). Of course, the fact that some words do give adults offence is precisely part of their appeal. And insofar as youngsters indulge in swearing in order to give offence, it is anti-social behaviour, and will be sanctioned by society accordingly. It is when swearing becomes invasive or abusive that we need to be worried. Groups that swear quietly among themselves bother no one.

Everybody swears. It is a natural response to an emotional state. Swearing is not so much a 'use' of language as an outburst, an explosion, which gives relief to a surge of energy. We can see this when we aim a swearword at an object rather than a person, such as when our head makes inadvertent contact with a low roof beam. Aimed at people, it is often a substitute for an aggressive bodily response, a handy means of avoiding physical conflict. We are wrong to look for much meaning in swearing. Phrases like *bleeding hell* are, literally, nonsense.

If we are politely brought up, and do think of the meaning of swearwords, then we will moderate them when we swear. Instead of *shit* we will say *sugar* or *shucks*. Instead of *God* we will say *gosh* or *golly* or *Gordon Bennett*. There is nothing new in such things. In Shakespeare's *Henry IV Part 1* (3.1.241), Harry Hotspur criticizes his wife for saying 'in good sooth', and launches into a tirade about how she swears 'like a comfit-maker's wife' with 'pepper-gingerbread' oaths. Everybody swears. It's just that they swear in hugely different ways.

Of course, just because some speakers don't find an expression taboo is no guarantee that their listeners won't. That is why there is so much concern about the use of swearing on radio and television. Broadcasters try to control it, by having 'watersheds' before which certain words are unacceptable. These are quite detailed, as the selection of items from one channel's list illustrates (*see* panel opposite). It is the racial terms that now warrant the gloss 'do not use at all'; traditionally offensive terms are less of an issue.

There is enormous uncertainty about the whole issue, because fashions in swearing change, as all language does, and what might be unacceptable to one generation turns out to be acceptable to another (*see* panel on p. 131). Swearing fashions vary from one part of the country to another too. In Caernarfon, in North Wales, you hear people calling each other *cunt* all the time, quite unconcernedly. It just means 'mate'.

Taboo on TV

This is a selection of words from one channel's guidelines:

bastard	definitely not before 8 p.m.; justified moderate use post 8 p.m.
bloody	fine any time
bugger	if used as in 'silly old bugger', OK anytime; if used with intent—not before 8 p.m.
cunt	post 10 p.m.; only in exceptional circumstances
fuck	post 9 p.m.
God	fine, but be careful of context/causing offence
nigger	not at all—must refer up [to senior management]
pissed off	6 p.m. onwards
shag	not before 9 p.m.
shit	6 p.m. onwards—moderate use
sodding	probably fine at any time
spastic	not at all; must refer up
twat	not before 9 p.m.
whore	not before 8 p.m.
yid	only if editorially justified

Part IV

The evolution of words

We examine the way the form and meaning of words evolve over time—the field of etymology. Vocabulary is always the most noticeable area of language change. So why do words come and go? How do they change their meaning? What changes are taking place today? Chapter 18 looks into the question of how individual words are created—an opportunity, it transpires, which is available to all of us. Chapter 19 looks at the other end of a word's life: the time when words become clichéd, archaic, and obsolete, and eventually die. Chapter 20 examines the whole process of language change, and maps the main ways in which the words of a language change their meaning over time. And Part IV closes with some thoughts about the future of words. Many people think the English language is in a state of decay, especially as new technologies—such as the mobile phone, with its idiosyncratic text-message abbreviations—make words change in unprecedented ways. What is this doing to vocabulary? The answer may surprise you.

18 **Wordbirths**

Can we be present at the birth of a word? The people attending a publishing trade association dinner in New York in 1907 were, though they didn't realize it at the time.

One of the publishers, B.W. Huebsch, had just published a successful book by the American humorist Gelett Burgess, *Are You a Bromide?* A *bromide* was Burgess's word for a dull, conventional person, and the book contained examples of current 'bromidioms' which would enable you to decide whether you were one or not (*see* panel overleaf). Free copies were given out to the people present, printed—as was the association's custom—in a special jacket.

The new jacket didn't satisfy Burgess. It was too conventional. The practice seen in contemporary lurid novels was a much better idea. There was always a damsel posing on the front cover. So he decided to draw one. He sketched out a buxom blonde on one of the jackets, and labelled her Miss Belinda Blurb. The name caught on. Any excessive testimonial for a book, on front or back covers, was soon being called a *blurb*. In a little wordbook he wrote a few years later, he defined his own term:

1. A flamboyant advertisement; an inspired testimonial.
2. Fulsome praise; a sound like a publisher.

And we have had the word with us ever since. There is a blurb on the back of this book.

It is very unusual to be able to pinpoint a word's origins so precisely. Or the moment a word was first used in a particular sense. We can get close, as with *sputnik* and *ground zero* (*see* p. 4), but rarely more than that. The usual scenario is the total opposite. We have no idea when a word was created, or where, or by whom. The ultimate origins of all words are lost in the mists of time (*see* chapter 6). But even on a historical time-scale,

Ten bromidioms

This world is such a small place, after all, isn't it?

I don't know much about Art, but I know what I like.

I've had a perfectly charming time.

That dog understands every word I say.

It isn't money, it's the principle of the thing I object to.

If you'd only come yesterday, this room was in perfect order.

Now you have found the way, do come often!

No, I don't play chess. I haven't got that kind of a brain.

Funny how some people can never learn to spell!

I thought I loved him at the time, but of course it wasn't really love.

within a particular language, we have no idea. Who first used the word *cut* in Old English, or *help*, or *king*?

What we have, of course, is the first recorded use of a word. So, we can go to an unabridged *Oxford English Dictionary*, look up the word *king*—easily done, these days, on CD or online—and find the earliest text in which the lexicographers have discovered the word. And there it is, in Annal 488 of the Old English Chronicle, dated around 855 CE: 'In this year Æsc succeeded to the kingdom, and was king (in Old English, *cyning*) of Kent for 24 years'.

How long had *king* been in the language before it first came to be written down? Nobody knows. One word can be spoken for a considerable period of time before anyone bothers to write it. Another is felt to be so needed that it comes into written language virtually immediately. It will vary from period to period. In Old English we could be talking centuries. In Shakespeare's time, decades. Today, thanks to the Internet, a few hours.

The Internet is changing everything, as far as lexicography is concerned. The World Wide Web is the biggest collection of written English there has ever been, and every word in it is either already indexed or capable of being indexed. Indexing doesn't only mean identifying the word-form. It means being able to say exactly when and where it appeared. You can see this process operating on your own computer, if you activate the appropriate software. My machine records that I changed a word in this paragraph at 6.45 p.m. on 10 August 2005. And if I put this text on the Internet, everyone else would know it too.

So, if I were to invent a new word now—*debagonization*, say (*see* p. 25)—and put it on my website, it would be in the public written domain in a way that would have been inconceivable twenty years ago. Browsing lexicographers might then spot it and note it down. If it caught on, it would eventually get into their dictionaries. If I was a wordsmith, I might shortcut the whole process by sending in the new word myself (*see* 'Becoming a word detective', 3). Either way, the birthday of the word will be known.

We can see wordbirths also in the occasional word coinage competition. 'Invent a word that we need' is the simple instruction—and people do! When I played this game with listeners during my *English Now* series for Radio 4 back in the 1980s, I was expecting a few dozen entries, and I got over a thousand. Some of the best creations are in the panel overleaf. I'm not expecting them to become a permanent part of the English language, but you never know.

Some wordbirths are especially interesting—those introduced by famous authors, in particular. Here the birthdate is conventionally taken to be the date of publication of the work. So, we can work our way through the innumerable coinages in James Joyce's *Finnegans Wake* (*weilderfight*, *penisolate*, *rearrived* . . .) and assign them all to 1939—or to the previous seventeen years during which the book was in progress. In the case of Shakespeare, the dating is more uncertain, but the principle is the same.

New words?

blinksync *noun* The guarantee that, in any group photo, there will always be at least one person whose eyes are closed.

circumtreeviation *noun* The tendency of a dog on a leash to want to walk past poles and trees on the opposite side to its owner.

hicgap *noun* The time that elapses between when hiccups go away and when you suddenly realize it's happened.

kellogulation *noun* What happens to your breakfast cereal when you are called away by a fifteen-minute phone call just after you have poured milk on it.

potspot *noun* That part of the toilet seat which causes the phone to ring the moment you sit on it.

Shakespeare, the uncrowned king of word creation. Or perhaps the *Oxford English Dictionary* (OED) did in effect crown him, by attributing more word 'first recorded instances' to him than to any other author. Of course, just because you are the first person recorded as using a word does not mean that you invented it. The swear words *'sblood* ('God's blood') and *'slid* ('God's eyelid') are illustrated from his plays, but they are hardly his inventions. They are simply the sources the lexicographers chose to illustrate the use of these words.

But there's something different about words like *anthropophaginian* and *exsufflicate*. They suggest a personal touch. And when we see clusters of interesting word-formations appear, then we can sense an individual author's hand: *out-Herod*, *outfrown*, *outpray*, *outswear*, *outvillain* . . . In all there are 2,035 'first usage' words in the OED assigned to Shakespeare. My estimate is that about 1,700 of these are imaginative coinages on his part. An amazing total, by any standards.

And even more amazing is the impact of these words on the subsequent development of the language. About half of them fell out of use—words

Williamisms

A selection of words whose first recorded use in the *Oxford English Dictionary* is assigned to Shakespeare. It is a matter of judgement which of these are everyday uses, which Shakespeare happened to use, and which are genuine coinages on his part.

. . . *chaffless, chaliced, champion* (as a verb), *changeful, channel* (as a verb), *chanson, chapless, characterless, cheerer, cheese-paring, chidden, childness, chimney-top, chop-fallen, choppy, churchlike, Cimmerian, circummure, climate* (as a verb), *clod-poll, closing* (as an adjective), *clot-poll, cloud-capped, cloyless, coign, cold-hearted, collected, collied, combless, co-mingle, committed, commutual, companion* (as a verb), *compassion, compelling* (as an adjective), *comply, compunctious* . . .

There is a complete listing of all Shakespeare's first recorded uses in *The Shakespeare Miscellany* (*see* 'Becoming a word detective', 8). The term *Williamism* is used in my articles on Shakespearean lexical innovation in *Around the Globe*, the magazine of Shakespeare's Globe theatre in London.

like *substractor, incardinate*, and *vizament*. But that leaves some 800 clear-cut cases, such as *abstemious, accessible*, and *assassination*, which achieved a permanent place in English, as well as around a hundred idiomatic expressions, such as *fair play* (from *Troilus and Cressida*) and *pomp and circumstance* (from *Julius Caesar*). Shakespeare remains a key innovator in the history of the language.

So, when we talk about wordbirths we are not just talking about birthdates. On a lexical birth certificate we need to say who the mother or father were, and where the happy event took place. Shakespeare, it seems, had about 800 lexical children. Most modern authors, I imagine, would be pleased enough if they had given birth to just one.

19 **Worddeaths**

We can sometimes date the birth of a word, but we can never date its death. For when is a word dead? Presumably when nobody uses it any more. But when can we be sure that people are no longer using a word? How much time should we allow to go by before we can say that a word has stopped being *obsolescent* (in occasional use by a few) and become *obsolete* (used by no one)?

Let's take a clear case: *frumsceaft*, meaning 'creation'. This is an Old English word, used by the Anglo-Saxons, most famously when Caedmon had a mystical vision. He was an unlettered cowherd, living sometime in the seventh century, who became England's first Christian poet. The story is recorded in Bede's *Ecclesiastical History*.

Caedmon tells how he would be sitting in the beer-hall at a banquet, when the harp was passed around for people to sing—that is, sing poetry. He didn't know any poems, he says, so he would get up when he saw the harp coming his way, and creep back to his cowshed. Then one day he had a dream in which a man calls out to him: 'Caedmon, sing me something.' He replies, 'I don't know how to sing, and that's why I left the banquet.' The dream-man says, 'But you can sing for me.' 'What shall I sing?' asks Caedmon. 'Sing me frumsceaft', says the voice. So Caedmon does. And we have the first recorded Old English poem.

Frumsceaft lasted until the arrival of the French, when the Romance word eventually took over. We don't know who used it last. But we find the first recorded use of *creation* in 1393. *Frumsceaft* went out of use. Nobody uses it now, unless of course quoting passages from Old English, or using the Wikipedia website, which is trying to make Old English a cool subject once again (*see* 'Becoming a word detective', 8).

The evolution of words

Inwit is apparently another such case. In Old English it meant 'evil, deceit'. Then in Middle English it appears in the language a second time, now in the sense of 'conscience' or 'reason'; the first recorded usage is 1225. But the French incomers preferred the originally Latin word *conscience*, which is also recorded from that date. Indeed, the two words are linked together, one glossing the other, in an early Middle English religious text called the *Ancrene Riwle* ('way of life for anchorites').

Throughout the Middle Ages the two words competed for a place in the language. And *conscience* won. *Inwit* was still occasionally being used into the sixteenth century—there is a usage recorded as late as 1587—but then it dies out.

Or does it? In the nineteenth century, some writers with an enthusiastic nostalgia for Anglo-Saxon times began to use it again. William Barnes was one (*see* p. 50). In 1922 the poet Robert Bridges called for the rehabilitation of 'good Old English words' such as *inwit*. James Joyce used it in *Ulysses*. Ezra Pound used it. In *The Listener* in 1968, the fans of James Bond were thought 'to be able to turn a blind eye to the bites and agenbites of new-Bond's *inwit*'—the allusion is to a medieval text called *The Agenbite of Inwit* ('the remorse of conscience').

This evidence of revival—or perhaps better, resurrection—is taken from the pages of the *Oxford English Dictionary*. It is enough to say that the word is by no means dead, even though it tends to live on only in italics, or in a glossed form, showing the reader that there is something special about it. Has it any real life? It has been artificially resuscitated by literary types, certainly, but is that enough to say it is alive again? Or is it a lexical zombie, awaiting the moment when people lose interest, and it can return gratefully into its grave?

Other old-fashioned words—linguists call them *archaisms*—have much more of a natural life. You and I might not spontaneously use *inwit*, but we might well use *damsel*, *hither*, *varlet*, and *forsooth*—to take just a few examples found in some recent children's stories about medieval characters. It would be impossible to miss them if you were a fan of the film trilogy *Lord of the Rings*—and most people seem to be. But you don't have to read a book or go to the cinema to encounter archaisms. Villages have their *olde tea shoppes*. Biblical or Shakespearean resonances turn up in newspaper headlines and television ads. *What doth it profit a man to gain the Dow Jones Industrial Average and lose his own soul?* began one business report in the 1990s.

Some recent archaisms

We do not have to go back as far as Elizabethan English or the Middle Ages to encounter archaisms. Here are some from the Victorian and Edwardian eras:

> *beastly* (as in 'so beastly critical')
> *blest, deuced* (if I know)
> *capital!* (as an exclamation of delight)
> *very civil* (of you)
> *confound you!*
> *damnable* (cheek)
> *guv'nor* (meaning 'father')
> *luncheon*
> *pray* (come in)
> (you) *rotter*
> *spiffing*

And might we not say that *daddy-o* is an archaism, even though it was alive and well in the 1960s?

We never know when an old word is suddenly going to reappear, often in a new sense. *Wireless* was comfortably dead, having been superseded by *radio*. Then it suddenly re-appeared, useful as a new-technology contrast with the cabled (*wired*) computer world, and generating a new set of forms, such as *wi-fi*. Old grammar and spellings can come alive again too, as we see with *doth* and *shoppe*. But it is old vocabulary that is most often employed in this way.

The evolution of words

Even if we don't know that a word is dead, there are several clues that tell us when a word is dying. Or at least, seriously ill. We judge a word's state of health by the things people say about it. When people start to condemn a word or expression as being overused, trite, or hackneyed, and take the trouble to send letters or emails complaining to the BBC or the *Daily Telegraph* about it, we know that something is up. We have a word for such living-dead expressions. We call them *clichés*.

The criticisms are understandable. The overuse of any word becomes irritating. If I really wanted you to become really annoyed with a particular word, all I would really have to do is really overuse it in a sentence, and you'd get really upset with me. Really. The word loses its meaning after a while. It becomes a habit, a nervous tic, and when that happens you would be right to say it ceases to mean anything much.

That is why people don't like clichés. Because they are overused, they lose their meaning, and they suggest that their users don't care much about meaning. We look approvingly on people who it seems are trying to be fresh and imaginative in their use of language, or who are trying to be clear, careful, and precise. Conversely, we criticize people who it seems are being lazy and unimaginative in their use of words. So, we would have little time for anyone who larded their speech routinely with expressions such as those shown in the panel opposite.

Because everyone condemns clichés—it is a snarl word (*see* p. 127)—it is a brave linguist indeed who stands up for them. I am one such. I have just one point to make, and that is that clichés often have a value. Their usefulness is to express precisely what the critics condemn. If we *wish* to be lazy or routine in our thinking, if we *wish* to avoid saying anything precise, then clichés are what we need. And such wishes are commonplace. It is not possible, or desirable, to be fresh and imaginative all the time.

Life is full of occasions when a serious conversation is simply too difficult, or too energetic, and we gratefully fall back on clichés. They can fill an awkward gap in a conversation. They can be a lexical lifejacket when we are stuck for something to say. Think of the passing remarks we make to people we know as we see them in the street, but with no time to stop and talk. Think of the required politeness of regular commuters on a train. Think of the forced interactions at cocktail parties. Or the desperate platitudes which follow a funeral. These are the kinds of occasion which give clichés their right to be.

In a nutshell

I compiled this piece of cliché-speak for a radio programme in the 1980s. I doubt if it holds the record for the longest cliché sequence ever, but it can't be far off.

If I may venture an opinion, when all is said and done, it would ill become me to suggest that I should come down like a ton of bricks, as large as life and twice as natural, and make a mountain out of a molehill on this issue. From time immemorial, in point of fact, the object of the exercise, as sure as eggs are eggs, has been, first and foremost, to take the bull by the horns and spell it out loud and clear. At the end of the day, the point of the exercise is to tell it like it is, lay it on the line, put it on the table—putting it in a nutshell, drop a bombshell and get down to the nitty-gritty, the bottom line. I think I can honestly say, without fear or favour, that I have left no stone unturned, kept my nose firmly to the grindstone, and stuck to my last, lock stock and barrel, hook line and sinker. This is not to beat about the bush or upset the apple cart, but to give the green light to the calm before the storm, to hit the nail on the head, to bite the bullet, and thus at the drop of a hat to snatch victory from the jaws of defeat.

That's it. Take it or leave it. On your own head be it. All good things must come to an end. I must love you and leave you. I kid you not. Don't call us, we'll call you. And I don't mean maybe.

Am I right or am I right?

We rightly complain when we encounter people using clichés in contexts where we expect better. A politician who answers a direct question with clichés can expect to be condemned. Clichéd responses by a student will not gain marks; clichéd comments by a radio journalist will not gain listeners. But a blanket condemnation of all clichés on all occasions is as futile as an unthinking acceptance. Clichés have been called 'Musak of the mind' and 'social lubrication'. Both views have truth in them.

20 **Wordchanges**

Words have no life of their own. It is people who have life, and it is they who give life to words. Or death. And as people, and their societies, never stand still, neither do words. Change is the norm. The only words that do not change any more are dead ones.

We looked at the history of one word, *nice*, in detail in chapter 6. Every word in the language has a comparable story to tell. Each story is unique. No two words have identical histories, and as a result no two words have identical meanings and ranges of usage. There are actually no true synonyms.

You can check this claim out easily enough by referring to the pages of a thesaurus, such as Roget's. That work was described in one edition as 'a collection of synonyms on a grand scale'. It isn't. Roget himself is much more circumspect, describing it in his Preface as a collection of words arranged 'not in alphabetical order as they are in a Dictionary, but according to the *ideas* which they express'. Indeed, he goes out of his way to say that he is not going to explain the 'signification' of words. Far less, he says, 'do I venture to thrid [= thread] the mazes of the vast labyrinth into which I should be led by any attempt at a general discrimination of synonyms'. It's been hard enough compiling the thesaurus as it is, he goes on to complain.

The difference between a dictionary and a thesaurus is clear. In a dictionary, we know the word and want to look up its meaning. In a thesaurus, we know the meaning, and want to look up the word. The panel overleaf shows a selection of words taken from one of Roget's categories. It is a fascinating and useful collection of words of closely related meaning—ideal for the budding author searching for 'the right word'. But it contains no true synonyms.

Young persons

Part of the section dealing with 'Young person' (section 132) in a 1960s edition of Roget's *Thesaurus*. The list includes additions to Roget's original list by the editor.

> *youngster, juvenile, young person, young hopeful; boy, schoolboy, stripling, adolescent; youth, callant, lad, laddie; urchin, nipper, shaver, whipper-snapper; codling, cub, unlicked cub; hobbledehoy, Teddy-boy; minor, master, junior, cadet; midshipman, cabin-boy, powder-monkey; buttons, call-boy, page-boy, servant; girl, schoolgirl, lass, lassie, missie, wench, maid, maiden, virgin; chit, chicken, chick, miss, young miss, junior miss; teenager, bobbysoxer, flapper, tomboy, hoyden, romp; giglet, minx, baggage; colleen, mademoiselle, damsel, damozel, nymph, nymphet.*

You might say: what about *youngster* and *youth*? Indeed, these are very close, but they are not identical. There are nuances associated with the one which we do not find with the other. Compare these two sentences, and you will sense them straight away:

> *There are some youngsters standing outside the house.*
> *There are some youths standing outside the house.*

Which group would worry you? *Youths* plainly has negative associations which are lacking in the case of *youngsters*. Youngsters are nice to know. Youths may not be.

But this is by no means the whole story. These are plural uses of the nouns. In the singular, *youth* is usually used in a positive way. The website *youth.org* describes itself as 'Resources and links for gay and lesbian youth to learn about their sexuality as well as provide a safe place to express themselves.' Nothing negative about that. And *youth* shows many other distinctive connections between words—linguists call them *collocations*—

such as *youth sports*, *youth groups*, *youth hostel*, and *youth culture*. *Youngster* doesn't typically have these collocations. And if one were to be used, it would mean something different. A *hostel for youngsters* would not be the same as a *youth hostel*.

Change in meaning—*semantic change*—is a fact of life. Love it or hate it, we can't stop it. We may regret the passing of a word, or a sense of a word, but we can only react to what has happened; we cannot stop it happening. Nor can we ever predict the way a word is going to change its meaning. Try now. Take any word on this page and say how it will change its meaning in five years' time. It is an impossible task. We can only ever be wise after the event, with words.

Wordsmiths spend as much of their lives as possible increasing their wisdom after the multifarious events of semantic change. They look for interesting word histories like bees look for nectar, settling on one source of information, extracting what they can, then moving on to another. *Lord* comes from *hlaford* in Old English, literally meaning 'loaf-keeper'. Bzzz. *Lady* comes from *hlafdig*, literally 'loaf-kneader'. Bzzzzzzz. Some wordsmiths even work in hives, under the leadership of a queen, or sometimes a king. Then they are called lexicographers (*see* chapter 5).

The study of bees is part of entomology. The study of the history of words is *etymology*. Being an etymologist is the most fascinating of professions—though without a day-job, as Eric Partridge used to say, it won't pay the mortgage. It is interesting, not just because of the individual word-histories, but because of the trends that can be discovered in the way words change their meaning.

Some words widen their meaning over the course of time. Words like *office* and *novice* were originally restricted to the field of religion. A priest would read his daily office. A new monastery or nunnery recruit would be a novice. Today, these senses form only a tiny part of the cluster of meanings that are conveyed by these words. When words expand their meaning in this way, etymologists call the process *extension* or *generalization*.

The opposite process also occurs, one of *narrowing* or *specialization*. *Engine*, for instance, was formerly used in the very general sense of 'mechanical contrivance'. Devices of war and of torture could be called engines. But since the Industrial Revolution, the word has come to mean

Why is there glamour in grammar?

Grammar, recorded since the early fourteenth century, is much older than *glamour*. It came into English via Old French and Latin, and ultimately from Greek, where *grammata* meant 'letters'. To the illiterate, *grammar* quickly came to be identified with the mysterious domain of the scholar, and thus developed the sense of 'learning' (in general), and then of 'the incomprehensible'. It was a short step from there to a sense of 'witchcraft' and 'black magic'.

Much later, in the 1720s in Scotland, a form of the word appears spelled with an *l*. The switch from *r* to *l* is common enough in English—we see it again in *purple* from *purpure* and *pilgrim* from *peregrinus*. This word kept its magical sense, to begin with. Robert Burns was one of the first to link the two, in 'Captain Grose's Peregrin' (1789):

> Ye gipsy-gang that deal in glamor,
> And you deep read in hell's black grammar,
> Warlocks and witches.

The resonances of darkness are still evidently there.

As other authors took it up, the word started to change its meaning. It is used by Walter Scott, Tennyson, and Charlotte Bronte, for instance, and we can trace a steady shift from 'witchcraft' to 'enchantment' to 'alluring charm'. In the twentieth century, 'good looks' were added to the mix, thus producing the *glamour boys* and *glamour girls* of the 1930s. *Glam* became popular slang. In the 1970s we find such bands as T Rex and Slade playing *glam rock* music. And just when the study of grammar was going out of fashion!

'mechanical source of power'. It has narrowed its meaning. So has *meat*, once used to mean 'food in general'.

Another trend is when a word takes on a positive sense of approval. If we say that a man is *lean*, we are likely to mean that he has a fit, athletic physique, and probably good looks. I typed *Brad Pitt* into Google, and there it was, first hit: 'Brad Pitt is lean, all legs and lips and liquid movement.' Etymologists call this kind of semantic development *amelioration*. *Revolutionary* is another word that has ameliorated over time—it is a good thing, if a product is advertised as 'revolutionary'. Not so in 1789.

And we find the opposite process: *deterioration*. A word develops a negative sense of disapproval. Middle English *villein* referred to a serf, honest, and hard-working. Modern *villain*, although often used jocularly, is quite the opposite. *Lewd* originally meant 'of the laity, not clerical'. In Modern English it has been entirely taken up with sexual impropriety.

This is where we have to be especially careful, when studying the language of earlier periods of English. When Wycliffe, for example, talks about *lewd freres* (*freres* = 'brothers'), he means only that they were lay-brothers, not ordained. It is of course the easiest thing in the world to read in the modern meaning of this phrase and think that the men were engaged in sexual antics.

Lewd in the Middle Ages and *lewd* today are 'false friends'. Believe it or not, that is a technical term in linguistics. It refers to words which seem to be the same, but are not. There are false friends between modern languages too. All English learners are temporarily fooled, when learning French, by *demander*. They think it means 'demand', and then find out that it means 'ask'. *Demander* and *demand* are false friends.

Students of Shakespeare have to learn to live with the false friends that separate Early Modern English from the language of today. *Bootless*, for instance, today means 'without boots'. This sense of the word is actually known from the fourteenth century; but it is not Shakespeare's normal usage, where it means 'uselessly, in vain'. The word is from Old English, where it meant 'good' or 'use' (*better* comes from the same root). So when Caesar addresses the company with 'Doth not Brutus bootless kneel?' (*Julius Caesar*, 3.1.75) or a fairy enquires of Puck 'Are not you he / That . . . bootless make the breathless housewife churn' (*A Midsummer Night's Dream*, 2.1.37), the issue is nothing to do with footwear.

Three more false friends

excrement

The word today means 'waste matter discharged from bowels', but in Shakespeare's time it had a second sense, meaning 'outgrowth'— as of hair, nails, or feathers. He is in fact the first to be recorded using the word in this way, when in *Love's Labour's Lost* (5.1.98) Don Armado boasts to Holofernes that the King 'with his royal finger thus dally with my excrement'. The modern reaction varies from giggling to disgust, until it is appreciated that here we have a false friend.

naughty

In modern English, the word means 'badly behaved' (of children), 'improper' (playfully, of adults), or 'sexually suggestive' (of objects, words, etc.). None of these meanings apply when Portia describes a candle flame in the darkness: 'So shines a good deed in a naughty world' (*The Merchant of Venice*, 5.1.91). Here the tone is serious, for the word meant 'wicked, evil, vile'.

revolve

For Shakespeare, the primary meaning was 'consider, ponder, meditate'. The modern sense of 'perform a circular motion' didn't come into the language until a century later. So when Malvolio reads the letter which tells him 'If this fall into thy hands, revolve' (*Twelfth Night*, 2.5.139), he shouldn't solemnly turn himself around, but simply look very thoughtful. If only modern actors and directors knew that! I have seen the play dozens of times, and never seen a production yet where the actor doesn't dutifully turn himself round.

'The memories of childhood have no order and no end', reflected Dylan Thomas in his nostalgic story 'Quite Early One Morning'. It is the same with etymology. The examples in this chapter have taken me in all kinds of unpredictable directions, and only the thought of a length-limit and a publisher's deadline has stopped me exploring further. You will find the same, if you allow your etymological inclinations to rule (*see* 'Becoming a word detective', 1). 'The judicious author's mind is enthralled by etymology', said Wordsworth, in the 1815 preface to the *Lyrical Ballads*. In that case, we are all judicious authors.

21 **Wordfutures**

How is the English language doing, at the beginning of the new millennium? What is the future of English vocabulary? Call forth the prophets of doom.

A comment from Lever Bros:
> It is a great surprise and disappointment to us to find that our young employees are so hopelessly deficient in their command of English.

A spokesman from Boots:
> Our candidates do not appreciate the value of shades of meaning.

And who to blame? This next writer is under no illusions:
> Look . . . at the process of deterioration which our Queen's English has undergone at the hands of the Americans. Look at those phrases which so amuse us in their speech handbooks; at their reckless exaggeration, and contempt for congruity; and then compare the character and history of the nation—its blunted sense of moral obligation and duty to man; its open disregard of conventional right where aggrandisement is to be obtained; and, I may now say, its reckless and fruitless maintenance of the most cruel and unprincipled war in the history of the world.

Oh, I'm sorry. Did I not say? These are not contemporary comments. The first two were made in 1921, and quoted in the Bullock Report on English in schools (1975). The last came from the opening of Dean Henry Alford's book *The Queen's English*, first published in 1864. He was talking, in case you were wondering, about the American Civil War.

My point is linguistic, not political. Every age has its pundits who reflect gloomily on the present state of the language, make dire prophecies about its future, and wish things were like the earlier golden age they remember so well. But there was never any golden age. Dean Alford and his correspondents looked back with nostalgia at the linguistic excellence of the century before. But what were the authors saying then?

> When I took the first survey of my undertaking, I found our speech copious without order, and energetick without rules: wherever I turned my view, there was perplexity to be disentangled, and confusion to be regulated.

That was Dr Johnson, in the Preface to his *Dictionary* in 1755. And the century before that? John Dryden gloomily reflects in 1672:

> That an Alteration is lately made in ours [language] since the Writers of the last Age (in which I comprehend Shakespear, Fletcher, and Jonson) is manifest.

And he means an alteration for the worse.

I could go on. Writers on usage in the sixteenth century were gloomy about the linguistic future. William Caxton in the fifteenth century was gloomy about the linguistic future. John of Trevisa, writing in the fourteenth century, was gloomy about the linguistic future. In fact, the only people who seem not to have been linguistically downhearted were the Anglo-Saxons. But then, they had other things to worry about, like marauding Vikings.

And the evidence, from age to age, is that the fears were unfounded. The writers in the Middle Ages who were so fearful of the effect of foreign words on English (*see* chapter 8) had not reckoned with the ability of a Shakespeare to use them to stunning advantage. Dean Alford did not have the opportunity to read Twain, Faulkner, and Steinbeck, to take just three of the American writers who have enriched our lives since his day. And contemporary commentators have not anticipated the brilliant writers of the twenty-first century, some not yet born, who will enrich the language yet again.

Languages do not improve or deteriorate. They just change, like the tides. Yesterday's tide is no better or worse than today's or tomorrow's. On Tuesday one part of the beach is more affected; on Wednesday it is another. Words come and go. Grammar fluctuates. Pronunciations alter.

Spelling preferences vary. None of it adds up to a doomsday scenario, notwithstanding the best efforts of media pundits to say that it does.

Take text-messaging, a development of the late 1990s which took mobile phones by storm in the early 2000s. Millions of texts are sent each day, especially by youngsters and the young at heart. The restriction of the phone screen to 160 characters soon motivated an abbreviated style of writing, full of rebuses (*C* for *see*, *l8r* for *later*). It became routine to drop vowels and punctuation marks, and add new symbols such as the emoticons, or smileys :).

Some observers were horrified. *C* for *see*? What will this do to English spelling? What will it do to children's ability to think, if they fall into the habit of using short messages? When it was noticed that some kids were trying out these new forms in their schoolwork, the pessimism was reinforced. The next generation would be unable to communicate intelligibly at all.

Five years on, and the new genre is settling into its linguistic place within society. It is in fact not as new a genre as all that. Rebuses have been around in language at least since Ancient Egyptian times, and most people have done some rebus puzzles in Christmas annuals when they were children. The supposed cognitive limitations of the new genre on thinking were solidly squashed by events like *The Guardian* Text Message Poetry Competition (*see* panel overleaf). And the daring extension of texting conventions to schoolwork was spotted and dealt with straight away by a cadre of professionals whose job it is to develop and maintain children's sense of stylistic appropriateness. They are called English teachers.

The key word is appropriateness. Texting language is totally appropriate for its setting, mobile phone technology. It is appropriate when it carries over into chatroom settings and instant messaging, where it saves enormous amounts of typing time. It is not appropriate in settings where radical constraints of space do not apply, such as school essays and textbooks, and where there is an expectation of formality and a respect for standard conventions. Dis knda thng wdnt B gd :-(in a txtbk—though doubtless there are already novels written entirely in this way. Conversely, the kind of language I am using in this book would be entirely inappropriate for a mobile phone or chatroom.

New genres add to the expressive potential of a language. There is a literary effect in the previous paragraph, when I switched from conventional orthography to text messaging. I hope you liked it. But obviously this would not have been possible if the texting genre hadn't come into existence. And it is the same for all new genres. They allow authors to manipulate them in creative ways.

Winners from THE GUARDIAN Text Message Poetry Competition

I left my pictur on th ground wher u walk
so that somday if th sun was jst right
& th rain didnt wash me awa
u might c me out of th corner of yr i & pic me up
(*Emma Passmore*)

seasnd w msts n fruitlss mellwnss
n pungent smlls f grss ovr hay
we flp nto ponchos fr a mnts rest
n try nt t pln t rst f t day
(*Graham Francis*)

Jus left th clinic
bstrong cheri
arm ok no panic
need u 2 promis me
2 keep kissin
me left breast
cos baby nxt week
me right'll b missin
(*Peter Wroe*)

Take large prose texts, such as novels. Once the convention of using chapters is established, an author can depart from it, as does Lawrence Sterne in *Tristram Shandy*. His Chapters 18 and 19 of Book 9 have no text in them at all! Or take poetry. Once a sonnet of fourteen lines of ten syllables each is established, with a particular rhyme scheme, authors have the option of writing sonnets of different numbers of lines, or of varying the rhyme scheme. Look at Shakespeare's sonnet 126, twelve lines in couplets. Or sonnet 99: fifteen lines. Or Sonnet 85, with eight-syllable lines.

New words do the same. When a word enters the language, it comes in at a certain stylistic level, with a meaning and range of use that makes it fit within a particular variety. Then the situation changes, and it develops new nuances, word connections, and stylistic resonances. During the 1990s, for example, we acquired a large number of words to do with the domain of computing. Some of these were technical notions, such as *applet*, *blog* (or *weblog*), *cybernaut*, *screen saver*, and *spam*. Others were colloquialisms, such as *geek*, *nerd*, *ack* ('acknowledge'), and *nak* ('don't acknowledge' = 'I don't understand'). What is interesting is to observe the way the technical terms add senses, as they develop more colloquial uses. We have already seen this happening in the case of *404* (*see* p. 7), and there are dozens more cases like it (*see* panel overleaf).

All words eventually change. Sometimes the changes are simply a reflection of developments in culture or technology, as in the huge increase in the uses of *electronic* during the century. At other times the words extend figuratively, as in the case of *escalator*, originally a trade-marked product-name in 1900, which developed a use as a verb by 1920 ('to rush up a quickly moving stair'), and then several general senses. *Escalation* developed the meaning of 'incremental succession' in the 1930s, first in such contexts as the arms race, then in economic contexts with reference to prices and wages. A similar verb *to escalate* (as in *the crisis is escalating*) came a couple of decades later.

A book like *Twentieth-Century Words* (*see* 'Becoming a word detective', 1) displays the many different directions in which words come and go over a

Some extended meanings in computer language

bug

original use: 'error in a computer program or a fault in hardware'

extended use: 'hang-up, personality problem', as in *I'm afraid Jim still has a few bugs when it comes to dealing directly with clients*

download

original use: 'transfer information from one kind of electronic storage to another'

extended uses: 'receive all the news', as in *It'll take me a while to download everything you've said*; 'tell all the news', as in *It's my turn to download now*

online

original use: describing a peripheral device directly connected to a computer, or a computer directly connected to a site or network

extended uses: 'ready for anything, always around', as in *Sure Jon was at the party; he's one of the most online guys I know*; 'clued up, on the ball', as in *That's a really cool online remark*

relatively short period of time. Some words arrive prematurely, and only develop a significant use many years later. The word *television* was around in 1907 long before televisions were invented, and *motorway* was in use as early as 1903, though the first stretch of motorway was not built in Britain until 1958. Some words arrive late. In 1906 we find the first recorded use of *paedophilia*, previously, presumably, a deed without an explicit name. A surprising number of new words die—some scholars think as many as three-quarters of the coinages in a decade will not last. Examples of words which did not last beyond the first decade of the century include *marconigram* ('telegram'), *bovrilize* ('condense'), and *cerealist* ('someone who advocates a cereal diet').

There is so much going on, in any decade. In his little book *The Future of Swearing*, Robert Graves gives a perceptive definition of the future: it is, he says, 'only a view of the fantasticness of the present'. He was no prophet of doom. Each linguistic present is indeed a fantastic time.

Part V

WORDS

The enjoyment of words

The functions of words include enjoyment as well as communication. We all play with words, at some time or another, and enjoy the way in which others engage in wordplay. In the final chapters of the book, we see how this is done. Chapter 22 explores the ways in which words, viewed simply as patterns of sound, can delight or alienate. It suggests there could be meanings deep within the sounds of words. Chapters 23 and 24 look at how words can be a source of humour, entertainment, and social rapport. The examples turn out to be remarkably wide ranging. At one extreme they include the puns and jokes which sprinkle domestic conversation. At the other they include the highly crafted outputs of the professional advertiser, entertainer, or journalist. In between, we find the creations of the word-game enthusiasts, who range from opportunistic enthusiasts to total obsessives. Part V, and the whole book, then concludes with observations about the domain of literature, in which we experience lexical excellence at its best.

22 **Wordmelodies**

In 2004 the British Council carried out a survey to celebrate their 70th anniversary. They asked over 7,000 learners in forty-six countries what they considered to be the most beautiful words in English. They also ran an online poll on their websites abroad. Over 35,000 people voted. The top fifty results are shown in the panel below.

Beautiful words

These were the top fifty beautiful words in the British Council 2004 poll.

1	mother	18	hope	35	extravaganza
2	passion	19	grace	36	aqua
3	smile	20	rainbow	37	sentiment
4	love	21	blue	38	cosmopolitan
5	eternity	22	sunflower	39	bubble
6	fantastic	23	twinkle	40	pumpkin
7	destiny	24	serendipity	41	banana
8	freedom	25	bliss	42	lollipop
9	liberty	26	lullaby	43	if
10	tranquility	27	sophisticated	44	bumblebee
11	peace	28	renaissance	45	giggle
12	blossom	29	cute	46	paradox
13	sunshine	30	cosy	47	delicacy
14	sweetheart	31	butterfly	48	peekaboo
15	gorgeous	32	galaxy	49	umbrella
16	cherish	33	hilarious	50	kangaroo
17	enthusiasm	34	moment		

The enjoyment of words

This wasn't the first time there had been such an enquiry. In the 1970s, Terry Wogan got listeners to send in their words to his Radio 2 morning programme. And the *Sunday Times* held a similar competition in 1980. This was its top ten:

> *melody / velvet* (tied for first place), *gossamer / crystal* (tied for third place), *autumn, peace, tranquil, twilight, murmur, caress, mellifluous / whisper* (tied for tenth place)

And the list continued with such words as *caress, lace, lullaby, mellow, harmony*, and *eiderdown*. I do not know whether to be pleased or miffed at the result of the third-place tie.

Several wordsmiths in the US have also provided lists. This was lexicographer Wilfred J. Funk's top ten:

> *dawn, hush, lullaby, murmuring, tranquil, mist, luminous, chimes, golden, melody*

And this was the top ten from wordsmith author Willard R. Espy:

> *gonorrhea, gossamer, lullaby, meandering, mellifluous, murmuring, onomatopoeia, shenandoah, summer afternoon, wisteria*

Gonorrhea will have caught your attention. Surveys of this kind tend to mix up two kinds of criterion: words that have beautiful sounds and words that have beautiful meanings. The people who voted for *mother* in the British Council survey were almost certainly thinking of a beautiful meaning, as were those who voted for such words as *freedom, liberty*, and *hope*. Espy, by contrast, was thinking chiefly of the sounds, and ignoring any nasty connotations. Many of the words in the *Sunday Times* results similarly seemed to be there for their sound and not their meaning:

> *parakeet, didgeridoo, chrysalis, chinchilla, bewildered, akimbo, ominous, sycamore, pomp, syllabub, vacillate, antimacassar, doppelganger, zoo*

The interesting question is: what makes a word sound attractive? Which English sounds most appeal to listeners? An analysis of the most popular words does show some patterns, though there would certainly be differences between those who speak English as a native language and those who have learned it as a foreign language.

It would seem that a word which has the following characteristics is likely to be perceived as beautiful:

it contains at least one *l* sound;
it contains a nasal sound, especially *m*;
it contains other continuant sounds, such as *r* and *s*;
it contains two or three syllables;
the consonants vary from syllable to syllable, as in **melo**d*y*;
the vowel sounds vary from syllable to syllable, as also seen in *m***elo**d**y**.

Let us turn these trends into some real examples. *Melody* is worth citing because it satisfies all the trends, as does *mellifluous* and *luminous*. *Lullaby* is close too—and is a word that turns up on everyone's lists.

Are there tests we can carry out, to see if these trends are valid? Here are some possibilities.

Imagine you had to write a love story using romantic names of London Underground stations. It is likely that it would include *Pimlico* and *Colindale* and exclude *Goodge Street* and *Wapping*. This says nothing about the romantic status of the places themselves, of course. I imagine it is just as possible to have a passionate assignation in Wapping as in Pimlico. But phonetically, they are worlds apart.

These trends also explain many names of aliens in science fiction stories (*see* chapter 6). Friendly aliens are more likely to have such names as *Osnomians* and *Alarians*, whereas unfriendly aliens are more likely to be called *Grataks* or *Borgs* (the latter from *Star Trek*). And unfriendly entities are more likely to have names which use the sounds that don't appear in the beautiful words list. Did you notice that, *mother* and *enthusiasm* aside (both there for their meanings), there are no *th*'s in any of the above lists? And the significance of that? Ask Darth Vader.

These are, of course, trends, not black-and-white distinctions. When we examine lots of cases, we find interesting combinations. It would seem that one or two hard-sounding consonants (like *k*, *g*, *d*) can be enough to neutralize the effect of soft-sounding consonants (like *l*, *n*, *w*), otherwise we could not explain how the bad guys can be named *Klingons* and *Daleks*.

The study of the aesthetic properties of a language's sounds is called, appropriately enough, *phonaesthetics*. It is a subject that is still in its infancy, but its potential for explaining what we feel about words is enormous. How words sound is an essential factor in deciding on brand names, for instance, especially those which are linguistic inventions rather than established words. If we were creating a new beauty product, we might find more success with such names as *Ramelon* or *Melavin* than if we went for *Takop* or *Spet*. Conversely, a product which wanted a coinage to sound tough or aggressive, such as the name of a gun or a sports car, would do best to avoid the former sounds and go for the latter.

Comic writers have worked in this way for a long time. When Desperate Dan gets into trouble with the objects in his world, the nonsense words exploding in large capital letters around him typically include such hard-nosed monosyllabic forms as *bop*, *yipes*, *whup*, and *spludge*. He would not be half as successful if all he could do was produce such noises as *leem*, *nole*, or *marang*.

Poets have known all this for generations. Let us leave the last word on the matter with Tennyson, in these lines from 'The Princess' (canto 7):

> Myriads of rivulets hurrying through the lawn,
> The moan of doves in immemorial elms,
> And murmuring of innumerable bees.

23 **Wordplay**

Everybody plays with language or enjoys language play. Everybody. Which is not to say that everybody likes every kind of language play.

Puns are a case in point. There have been some famous voices raised against puns. The most famous, probably, is John Dryden, who in his 'Defence of the Epilogue' defined puns (they were called *clenches*, in his day) as 'the lowest and most grovelling kind of wit'. Ambrose Bierce, in *The Devil's Dictionary*, is even more acerbic: 'A form of wit, to which wise men stoop and fools aspire.'

But there is no agreement about the matter. Dr Johnson hated them; but his biographer, James Boswell, admired them. 'A good pun', says Boswell, in chapter 61 of his *Life of Johnson*, 'may be admitted among the smaller excellences of lively conversation.' Not just 'smaller' and not just 'lively', either. In literature, puns turn up sometimes with great impact and in the most serious of contexts. 'Can sick men play so nicely with their names?', ripostes the King to dying John of Gaunt, who has just spent several lines punning on the word *gaunt* (in Shakespeare's *Richard II*, 2.1.84).

Puns certainly are a paradox. We do not laugh at them; we groan at them, and the louder the better. They exist to give us enjoyable linguistic pain. Edgar Allan Poe, who knew a lot about pain, comments in his *Marginalia* that 'the goodness of the true pun is in the direct ratio of its intolerability.' I always imagine Vincent Price, in one of his sinister film roles, relishing that word, 'intolerability', and subjecting some unfortunate on the rack to a barrage of puns.

Hit me again. And again. Those who are into puns trade off each other incessantly. They engage in a phenomenon which linguists sometimes call 'ping-pong punning'. Not especially technical-sounding, admittedly, but a term which vividly captures the way people take up a pun and try to outdo each other. Anyone can generate an outbreak of ping-pong punning among their friends by choosing their moment and dropping a pun into the conversation. If the topic turns to the way some cats were heard yowling in the street last night, introduce *What a catastrophe!* and you will soon get reactions from the company: *A catalogue of disaster, Why not use a catapult?, I think they had catarrh.*

Ping-pong punning lasts as long as there is language to let it last. Usually not very long. There are only so many words beginning with *cat-*, after all. Also, it will only begin if the circumstances are right. The punsters have to be people who know each other well, the situation has to be informal, and everyone has to be in the right mood. We can hardly imagine such a sequence succeeding in a job interview.

Why do so many people play with language in this way? It isn't a specifically English thing. Some languages seem to go in for puns more than others (French more than German, for example), and some dialects more than others (British more than American). Although there are some fine American punsters—such as Richard Lederer—there is something about the British sense of humour which Americans do not 'get', and puns play a major part in it. *Huh? Oh, that's a pun, right?* But nobody has yet found a language or a dialect that doesn't play with words some of the time.

Why? Because wordplay involves the bending and breaking of the rules of the language, and it appeals to something anarchic in our personalities, which appreciates the incongruous and the bizarre. We know very well that the cat-yowling situation was not a catastrophe, that no catapults would ever be involved, and that the animals did not have catarrh. In *The Last Essays of Elia*, Charles Lamb put his finger on it when he commented, 'A pun is not bound by the laws which limit nicer wit'. And the point applies to all kinds of wordplay.

The purpose of wordplay is not to be funny. It has much broader aims. It builds rapport. The *cat*-exchange was something everyone enjoyed.

It integrated everyone into the conversation. If you were there, and unable to think up a good *cat* pun, you might feel a bit excluded—but you could make up for it by being even more vociferous in your condemnation of the others.

Wordplay builds relationships, and can break them. 'A difference of taste in jokes', George Eliot writes in *Daniel Deronda* (book 2, chapter 15), 'is a great strain on the affections'. And the same point applies to wordplay. The moment that girl tells boy (or vice versa) to 'Stop using those stupid voices!', the end of the relationship is in sight.

What other kinds of wordplay are there? The list is extensive. Rule-bending and -breaking can take us in all kinds of directions. Wordplay, along with situational humour, is the stuff of comedy, and there seems no end to comic linguistic invention. The genres include jokes, riddles, comic alphabets (*A is for 'orses*), dialect humour (*see* p. 107), fantastic word creation (p. 140), and nonsense words (p. 69). There are *spoonerisms*, which transpose sounds: *dear old queen* becomes *queer old dean*. There are *malapropisms*, which use similarities in pronunciation to mix up words: 'Her husband has a marvellous infection to the little page', says Mistress Quickly, in *The Merry Wives of Windsor* (2.2.112). She means *affection*. Malapropisms long antedate Richard Sheridan's character Mrs Malaprop (in *The Rivals*, 1775). Several of Shakespeare's comic characters use them.

The process starts young. Children start playing with words as early as three. Here's a transcript of a fragment of monologue from one three-year-old, on her own, playing with some animal toys. You have to imagine the words being half chanted, sometimes, as the chatter rambles on:

> *you're going on the bus, on the bus, on the bussy-bus . . . beep-beep, beepy bus, beepy sleep, sleepy bus . . . beep-a-deep-a-deep . . . beepy boop . . . boop-boop . . .*

The whole monologue went to and fro like this for half an hour. If there was ever evidence needed that we have an instinct for wordplay, it will be found in monologues like these. A little older, of course, and the play becomes more conscious and sophisticated. Knock-knock, anyone? There are a lot of these. I have a book called *1000 Jokes for Kids*. I have its companion: *Another 1000 Jokes for Kids*. Any parent has been through the mill of being told these jokes, interminably. *Mill* is the wrong metaphor. Edgar Allan Poe could provide some more apt ones.

Amateurs excel in wordplay, but they cannot beat the professionals: people who get paid for playing with words. They include newspaper editors searching for the clever headline and advertisers wanting the most memorable slogan. *Pain Stops Play*, was the headline reporting a cricket match where a batsman had to withdraw because bitten by an adder. It's effective—as long as you understand the allusion. You have to know that the traditional cricketing headline is *Rain Stops Play*. If you don't know

Catalysts

With wordplay, the more rules that are simultaneously broken, the more powerful the effect, as literary authors well know (*see* chapter 25). Here is an ingenious combination of pun and slogan, encountered as an article heading in the *Sunday Times* in 2005.

> Death is nothing new for TV, but Six Feet Under has refreshed the parts other biers cannot reach.

The pun totally relies on your knowledge of the Heineken slogan of the 1970s: *Heineken refreshes the parts other beers cannot reach.* Heineken in its day achieved one of the longest running campaigns in advertising by ringing the linguistic changes on its own slogan:

> Heineken refreshes the pilots other beers cannot reach.
> Heineken refreshes the pirates other beers cannot reach.
> Heineken refreshes the poets other beers cannot reach.

And now other people are doing the same thing to *it*. It is the highest linguistic accolade, of course, when your slogan becomes a catch-phrase, and is taken for granted by other writers.

this—and most Americans, for example, would not—the point is missed. Likewise, Brits on the whole would fail to grasp any puns deriving from baseball in headlines in the US press.

Most linguistically playful headlines are like that. And the same applies to ads which rely on wordplay. They make sense only to the culturally initiated. If you do not understand the original language, you will fail to pick up that a rule is being bent or broken. IBM was making a (probably safe) assumption about its intended audience's awareness of Descartes' *Cogito ergo sum* when it coined *I think, therefore IBM*. Slogans often allude to other slogans, in their wordplay. *Safety fast* was one for MG in the 1930s, standing on the shoulders of the famous accident-prevention slogan *Safety first*, first used in Britain sixty years earlier.

Wordplay has one other purpose: to be enjoyable in its own right. Most wordplay communicates next to nothing, by way of information about the real world. It is purely linguistic fantasy. *What is a vixen? A lady vicar*. It isn't, of course, but that is not the point. It is ludic linguistics. In this respect, wordplay moves us in the direction of other uses of language to be enjoyed in their own right, such as word games and literature.

24 **Wordgames**

Consider Scrabble. A word grid game. One of the most successful games in the history of the planet. Translated into all sorts of languages. And based on a simple premise which is linguistically crazy.

Scores are given to letters, and thus to words, and the highest score wins. We don't even need to know the meaning of the words we create. All that matters is that we get a good score. There are even books to help us win at Scrabble containing all the high-scoring two-letter words, three-letter words, and so on. XI, KA, ZO . . . How many of them do you know the meaning of? And, if you're in the middle of a game, do you really care?

Whoever could have come up with such a mad idea! That is not how we communicate. We do not, when talking to each other, mentally score our sentences. *That was a fine relative clause: I give it 18!* People do not hold up scorecards for words, as in an ice-skating competition. *Excellent word, premise. 9!* So why should we do it when playing a game?

Because it's fun. It appeals to something deep within us. And if I'd had the sense to think it up instead of becoming a linguistics academic, I would probably by now have earned enough in royalties to maintain all the dying languages of the world as well as my four children.

What does it appeal to? Linguistic wordgames are so popular because everyone can play them with minimal special skills. Wordgames based on speech are the easiest of all, because we learn to speak naturally. Hence we can all play games like *Blankety Blank* (Fill the blank: AUSPICIOUS — ?), without any extra training. Wordgames based on writing are a bit trickier, because we first have to learn to read, write, and spell; but once that is done, we are all on the same playing field. It isn't like *Mastermind*, where we have to assimilate huge chunks of extra knowledge; or the *Krypton Factor*, where we also have to be fit.

To play a wordgame, all we have to do is know our language. That is why there are so many game shows on radio and television. Anyone can play. They are supremely egalitarian. And, from a production point of view, they are cheap.

But it is still unusual behaviour. And all wordgames are the same. Consider crosswords, another grid game. Here is a situation where I want you to give me the answer to a question, but I am going to do my utmost—in the form of cryptic clues— to make sure you don't succeed. *These tokens are all of the same type (3 letters).*[1] Excuse me?

Those who set crossword puzzles know exactly what they are doing. You can tell by noting their professional names. Torquemada. Ximenes. Azed. Leaders of the Spanish Inquisition. Azed? Deza backwards. They are linguistic torturers. And the delight of doing a difficult crossword in X minutes is knowing that their efforts have been in vain.

You may already be a wordgame enthusiast, and spend your spare hours working out how many words you can make up out of the word set by your daily newspaper. My wife has extracted twenty words from today's challenge, PEDAGOGUE. The letter G has to appear in all of them, and all words have to be four letters or more. Her mother has managed twenty-one. Or you can play Scrabble, Boggle, Bandersnatch, Bookworm, and a hundred more published wordgames. These days, you can download versions of many of them onto your home computer. And if you do have an Internet connection, you can play against people from all over the world, or try and beat a computer opponent.

You can join wordgame clubs, or enter national and international wordgame competitions. Have you ever been involved in a major word competition, such as the Scrabble World Championships? Television

1 the

The enjoyment of words

coverage of one such tournament had a commentary that was a cross between the hushed tones of snooker (*He's going to play his Z . . . He's playing his Z . . .*) and the worst moments in a tennis match (*He's challenging the word. He's gone to the umpire—and she's not allowing it. Well, he's not at all happy . . .*). I've never actually seen anyone throw their tiles to the ground and howl, 'You can't be serious!', but I wouldn't be at all surprised to learn that it happens.

There is a drive within all wordgame enthusiasts to better themselves— which means upping the ante, as far as game difficulty goes. Take *lipograms*—texts constructed without using a particular letter of the alphabet. Not at all difficult if the letter to be omitted is Q. There isn't a single letter Q in the previous paragraph, for example. So, to make the challenge worth meeting, lipogram constructors go for the most frequently occurring letters of the alphabet, which in English are E, T, A, I, N, O, and S, in that order. E is the real challenge, obviously.

The task is: construct a sentence without the letter E. Not as easy as it seems, because you cannot use *the*, or regular past tenses (ending in *-ed*), or such common verbs as *are*, *were*, and *have*. But within a few seconds, most people would be able to put together something like *A tall man sat on a hill and had a sandwich*. So that is no challenge. But how's about this: write a poem of at least twenty lines without the letter E. Or: write a novel without the letter E.

Ernest Vincent Wright did just that, in 1939—a 50,000-word novel called *Gadsby*, without using a single letter E. Can such language sound natural, with two-thirds of the words in the language eliminated? You be the judge (*see* panel opposite). Some years later, Georges Perec did the same thing for French, in *La disparition* (1969)—a much harder task, given the greater use of E in French. It was translated into English by Gilbert Adair as *A Void*.

Some wordplayers find lipograms boring. Give me a real challenge, they say. So they go in for *univocalics*—texts in which only one vowel can be used throughout. Again, a short sentence isn't difficult to compile. *I sit in this bin, idling, sighing . . .* It might be a line from Samuel Beckett. The

Lipogrammatic novels

From the opening of *Gadsby*:

Upon this basis I am going to show you how a bunch of bright young folks did find a champion; a man with boys and girls of his own; a man of so dominating and happy individuality that Youth is drawn to him as is a fly to a sugar bowl. It is a story about a small town . . .

From Gilbert Adair's translation of *A Void*

Noon rings out. A wasp, making an ominous sound, a sound akin to a klaxon or a tocsin, flits about. Augustus, who has had a bad night, sits up blinking and purblind. Oh what was that word (is his thought) that ran through my brain all night, that idiotic word that, hard as I'd try to put it down, was always just an inch or two out of my grasp . . .

trick is to keep the language flowing when the task demands increase. Write a sonnet with only one vowel. You find that easy? All right then, write a story with only one vowel. Still easy? Well write a story in which every word *begins* with the same vowel. And, to add some spice, make it the story of *Hamlet*, or the story recounted in the *Book of Genesis*. Now that's a real challenge. And that is exactly the sort of task that wordgame enthusiasts will spend dozens of hours solving (*see* panel overleaf).

In 2002, Mark Dunn took the genre a stage further, by writing a 'progressive lipogrammatic' novel, *Ella Minnow Pea*. This tells the story, through correspondence, of the people of Nollop, who worship the author of the sentence *The quick brown fox jumps over the lazy dog*. When the Z falls from the monument they've erected to their hero, Nollop's priests interpret this as a divine commandment, and outlaw the writing or speaking of any word containing Z. Then Q falls. Then J. Chapter by chapter, the alphabet shrinks. Can the islanders save themselves from being silenced for ever?

And all abode 'appily

In a 1981 issue of the wordgame magazine *Word Ways*, there was this remarkable piece, based on the *Book of Genesis*. All words had to begin with the letter A. So how would the author get round the problem of Eve, let alone the Serpent?

Adam and alert associate, agreeably accommodated, aptly achieved accord and amiability—ample ambrosias available, and arbors alone adequate against ambient airs. Ah, auspicious artlessness! Adversity and affliction attacked appallingly, as avowed antagonists, Adonai, almighty Author, announced, and Apollyon, archangel-adder, asserted. 'Avoid apples and abide amid abundance,' admonished Adonai. 'Admire apples and acquire acumen,' advised Apollyon. Alas! Apollyon attained ascendancy. Ancestor Adam's attractive associate ate, arch and alluring against an antinomian apple-tree. Adam ate also, amoral although aware . . .

Wordgames start as fun and often become serious. They attract everyone from the mildly interested to the obsessive. A 50,000-word novel with no letter E? Why on earth??? The answer is the equivalent of the mountaineer's 'Because it's there'. To see if it can be done.

25 **Wordmasters**

On one of his journeys around the British Isles, the nineteenth-century traveller George Borrow fell in love with gypsy life, and began to learn Romani. His progress was so good that his tutors called him *Lav-engro*, 'Word Master'.

Wordmastery has two interpretations. The first is the linguistic sense. I am a master of words if I understand them and how they are used. That is what this book has been about. The second is the literary sense. I am a master of words if I use them well, and create works of art with them. Literature, as John Carey has recently reminded us (in *What Good are the Arts?*, 2005), is 'writing I want to remember—not for its content alone, as one might want to remember a computer manual, but for itself: those particular words in that particular order'. Bearing in mind our Anglo-Saxon oral wordhoards (*see* chapter 2), we might want to add: 'writing or speaking'. But the thrust of the observation is, to my mind, perfect.

I could fill the whole of this final chapter with quotations from our best authors affirming the centrality and memorability of words. I satisfy myself with W.H. Auden, writing in the *New York Times* in 1960: 'A poet is, before anything else, a person who is passionately in love with language.' The switch from *words* to *language* is very much to the point. Literature, said Anthony Burgess, in *A Mouthful of Air*, is 'the aesthetic exploitation of language'. That is, all aspects of language—sounds, spellings, grammar, vocabulary, patterns of discourse. This book has been predominantly about vocabulary, but authors do not live by vocabulary alone.

'Exploitation' is the key. Several times, over the last two chapters, I have talked about authors 'bending and breaking' the rules of language. The metaphor is not mine. It is Robert Graves's, who used it in a letter to *The Times* in 1961. 'A poet', he said, 'must master the rules of grammar before he attempts to bend or break them.' He might have added: the rules of vocabulary too, or any of the other features of language.

The enjoyment of words

That is what authors do: they bend and break linguistic rules. In all authors, deep down, there is a fear of banality. Of being accused of linguistic unoriginality. 'We've heard that before.' 'The language is full of clichés.' All authors try to avoid such charges by trying to be linguistically fresh. And the best way of doing that is to bend and break the rules, to depart from the normal ways in which people express themselves in conversation.

A poem illustrates one basic way of breaking rules. We do not normally speak in lines, or write in lines. Nor do we speak or write in lines of fixed length, with regular rhythm, or with rhyme. 'You've been a poet and you don't know it!' is a cat-call among children. They sense the abnormality when we rhyme inadvertently. Poetry relies on special linguistic constraints, and thus departs from the rules of everyday conversation, where these constraints are absent.

The more linguistic constraints that are built into the poetry, the more the author has to rise to meet the challenges they provide. It is a different kind of wordgame (*see* chapter 24), but a wordgame nonetheless, in which the ludic motivation is replaced by the aesthetic. Why try to write a poem in three lines of five, seven, and five syllables? The original motivation of the discipline lies in Zen Buddhism, but for many contemporary haiku writers in English, the answer is similar to that given at the end of chapter 24: not just 'to see if it can be done', of course—for a century of haiku-writing in English has demonstrated its brilliance as a literary form—but to rise to the challenge of mastering the discipline and doing it well.

Robert Frost, in a speech in 1935, made a wry comment about the need for poetic discipline: 'Writing free verse', he said, 'is like playing tennis with the net down.' Free versifiers would probably riposte by saying that they play with a different kind of net. But some sort of linguistic net there must be, whether we are talking about literature in poetry or in prose.

Prose texts share many rule-breaking strategies with poetry. Both genres manipulate sentence structure, vary word order, invent new words, devise idiosyncratic spellings, introduce unexpected connections between words, exploit the sound associations between words, and generally use all the devices of wordplay (*see* chapter 23). Most authors do only a few of these things at a time. After all, if every rule is broken at once, the task of understanding the text increases dramatically in complexity. Cue *Finnegans Wake*, where James Joyce does precisely that (*see* panel below). The fascination lies in the decoding.

An extract from FINNEGANS WAKE

(Anna Livia Pluribelle chapter):

Tell me, tell me, how cam she camlin through all her fellows, the neckar she was, the diveline? Casting her perils before our swains from Fonte-in-Monte to Tidingtown and from Tidingtown tilhavet. Linking one and knocking the next, tapting a flank and tipting a jutty and palling in and pietaring out and clyding by on her eastway. Waiwhou was the first thurever burst? Someone he was, whuebra they were, in a tactic attack or in single combat. Tinker, tilar, soulrer, salor, Pieman Peace or Polistaman. That's the thing I'm elways on edge to esk.

Literature presents us with a new linguistic world. Or rather, worlds. Because it is reflective of all human experience, it incorporates everything we have been talking about in this book. There is no subject-matter, or style of language, which is in principle excluded from the domain of literature. Authors can talk or write about whatever they want using whatever words they want. Depending on the climate of the times, there may be constraints—such as considerations of decency or blasphemy—but the contrast with the other uses of vocabulary described in this book is clear.

Whatever else we may say about literature, there is patently no way in which we can ascribe to literary works the kind of situational identity which can be given to the distinctive words of regional dialects, social genres, and occupational varieties, as described in Part III. Literature transcends this kind of constraint. Authors are free to circle above the dictionary, to swoop down and take from it whatever they wish. And to add to it whenever they wish. The language of literature has no situational restrictions. All words are available to it as a resource. And because there is no theoretical limit to the subject matter of literature, there is no theoretical limit to the words which authors may choose to employ.

The notion of a 'literary vocabulary' is therefore a nonsense. There have of course been certain words and expressions which we associate with the literature of different periods—poetical words such as *wight* and *o'er*— but these play only a tiny role in the gigantic corpus we call literature. Literature revitalizes the whole wordhoard. It refreshes the parts no other language variety can reach.

Although literature cannot be identified *by* language, it is wholly identified *with* it, for it has no other medium of expression. And vocabulary plays a central role in this identity, simply because there is so much more of it than anything else. We speak English using a tally of only some forty-four contrasting sounds, write with just twenty-six letters, incorporate a couple of dozen punctuation marks, build words from merely a few hundred elements, and construct sentences out of some 3,000 or so constructions—but we insert into these sentences the best part of a million words (*see* chapter 2). This is a different order of magnitude. It would take battalions of wordsmiths to report on them. The study of words has indeed no order and no end.

One of the best poems about words ever written, to my mind, is by Emily Dickinson (number 1212 in the *Collected Works*):

A word is dead
When it is said,
Some say.
I say it just
Begins to live
That day.

The story of words cannot be told in one book. But even a small word-book, like this one, can help make words come alive.

Part VI

WORDS

Becoming a word detective

In this section, I suggest several ways in which you can take forward your interest in words. It includes a number of specific activities, as well as sources of information in books, journals, societies, and websites (all domain names were live in late 2005). It excludes professional societies, such as those available to teachers of English, and also academic courses, information about which will typically be found in university departments of English or Linguistics. The most important recommendation, of course, is to develop good observational skills: to be alert to the language you see and hear around you, wherever you see and hear it. The most important pieces of equipment for the wordsmith are eyes, ears—and a pocket notebook.

You need to have a good dictionary available. And by 'good' I mean up-to-date, both in its coverage and its treatment. For instance, a dictionary without well-chosen examples of usage is of limited value. And a dictionary more than five years old is seriously dated. Many people change their cars every couple of years, and read the owner's manual avidly. Few people change their dictionaries in a decade, or ever read the dictionary preface. As a result, they fail to realize the power residing within the bonnet of their dictionary.

There is only one recommendation which outranks the advice to get a good dictionary. Get two. I have over a hundred, and I use them all.

1 How to find out the history of a word

Get an etymological dictionary

Most dictionaries will give at least a brief indication of where a word comes from, but to follow the stages of development in a word you need to get hold of an etymological dictionary—one where the emphasis is on word origins, as opposed to the way words are used today (see Part IV).

The fullest source is the unabridged *Oxford English Dictionary* (OED), usually available in libraries in its twenty-volume incarnation, but now conveniently accessible on CD (version 3.1 available in 2005) or online. The online version is accessible (for free) through most public and university libraries; you can take a tour of the online version at: **http://www.oed.com/tour/**. The CD information is at: **http://oed.com/services/cd-rom/**. Other online sources are the *Online Etymological Dictionary*: **http://www.etymonline.com/**. The *Shorter Oxford Dictionary* provides a clearer overview of the lexical forest.

Major works include:

A Comprehensive Etymological Dictionary of the English Language, edited by Ernest Klein (Elsevier, 1971).

The Oxford Dictionary of English Etymology, edited by C.T. Onions (Oxford University Press, 1966).

The Barnhart Dictionary of Etymology, edited by Robert K. Barnhart (Wilson, 1988).

The Oxford Dictionary of Word Histories, edited by Glynnis Chantrell (Oxford University Press, 2002).

Some authors have made a name for themselves exploring the history of individual words. Any book by Eric Partridge is rewarding, but see especially his: *Origins: a Short Etymological Dictionary of Modern English* (Routledge, 1977) and *A Dictionary of Slang and Unconventional English* (first published in 1937; 8th edition, revised by Paul Beale, Routledge, 2002). Partridge worked mainly in the decades surrounding the Second World War. A more recent author is John Ayto, whose books include the *Bloomsbury Dictionary of Word Origins* (Bloomsbury, 2001) and *Brewer's Dictionary of Phrase and Fable* (17th edition, 2005, Orion). US slang is the subject of Robert L. Chapman (and others), *Dictionary of American Slang* (3rd edition, HarperCollins, 1998).

Explore a word a day
Wordsmiths who have other things to do might need to pace themselves, and a 'word a day' is a good way of doing it. You can choose the word yourself, or get someone else to do it for you. The OED will email you its choice, if you register:
http://www.oed.com/services/email-wotd.html. Several websites offer a word a day.

Collect new words yourself
Some books and sites collect new words as they appear in newspapers, magazines, and elsewhere. Look at John Ayto's *Twentieth-Century Words* (Oxford University Press, 1999) or his *Longman Register of New Words* (Longman, 1989), and note how he does it. Remember to record the whole sentence in which a word appears, or even more than this, if the context is important. And record the source in full, including author, title, date, and page. (See also 'Send in words' under section 3 below.)

Read a general account
For more discursive accounts of word history, read Geoffrey Hughes, *Words in Time* (Blackwell, 1988) or *A History of English Words* (Blackwell, 2005). If you want still more references, see the bibliography in my own books (p. 205) or the webzine 'Take Our Word For It':
http://www.takeourword.com/bibliography.html.

2 How to find out about the meaning of names

Join a society

Some societies are very wide-ranging in coverage, dealing with all aspects of the study of names, onomastics (*see* chapter 10). In the British Isles there is the Society for Name Studies in Britain and Ireland: **http://www.snsbi.org.uk/index.html**. In the US, the American Name Society: **http://www.wtsn.binghamton.edu/ANS/**, in Australia, the Australian National Placename Society: **http://www.anps.mq.edu.au/**, in Canada, the Canadian Society of Names: **http://geonames.nrcan/.gc.ca/info/cssn_e.php**, and in South Africa, the Names Society of Southern Africa: **http://www.osu.unp.ac.za/NSA.htm**.

Several specialize in place-name work. In the UK, for example, there are:

The English Place-Name Society:
http://www.nottingham.ac.uk/english/research/EPNS/

The Scottish Place-Name Society:
http://www.st-andrews.ac.uk/institutes/sassi/spns/

The Ulster Place-Name Society:
http://www.ulsterplacenames.org/

Read an introductory book

On the field as a whole:

Leslie Dunkling, *The Guinness Book of Names* (Guinness, 1995).

On place names, you have the choice of a dictionary treatment or a discursive account.

Becoming a word detective

Dictionaries:

A.D. Mills, *A Dictionary of English Place Names* (2nd edition, Oxford University Press, 1998).

John Field, *Place-Names of Great Britain and Ireland* (David and Charles, 1980).

Discussions:

Kenneth Cameron, *English Place Names* (Batsford, revised 1988).

Margaret Gelling, *Place-names in the Landscape* (Weidenfeld and Nicolson, 2000).

C.M. Matthews, *Place Names of the English-Speaking World* (Weidenfeld and Nicolson, 1972).

On personal names, you need to follow up both first names and surnames.

First names:

Julia Cresswell, *Bloomsbury Dictionary of First Names* (Bloomsbury, 1990).

Leslie Dunkling and William Gosling, *Everyman's Dictionary of First Names* (Dent, 1983).

Patrick Hanks and Flavia Hodges, *A Dictionary of First Names* (Oxford University Press, 1990).

An online resource is *Behind the Name*: **http://www.behindthename.com/**.

Surnames:

P.H. Reaney and R.M. Wilson, *A Dictionary of British Surnames* (Routledge and Kegan Paul, 2nd edition, 1976).

R.M. Wilson and Percy H. Reaney, *Dictionary of English Surnames* (3rd edition, Oxford University Press, 1995).

See also the resource guide at Modern British Surnames: **http://homepages.newnet.co.uk/dance/webpjd/index.htm**.

Don't forget the related field of genealogy. Good sources are the Federation of Family History Societies: **http://www.ffhs.org.uk/** and the Guild of One-Name Studies: **http://www.one-name.org/**.

Use the dictionary
Remember to take a place-name dictionary in your suitcase when you're travelling. There is nothing more interesting than looking up the name of the place you're passing through; and nothing more frustrating (to the wordsmith) than having left the dictionary at home. Look out for local place-name books, especially in tourist locations. I found a new one on my last visit to Cornwall: Craig Weatherhill: *Place Names in Cornwall and Scilly* (Wessex Books, 2005).

And look out for name-studies of more specialized areas. If you are interested in commercial names, for example, there is Adrian Room, *Encyclopedia of Corporate Names Worldwide* (McFarland, 2002). Every field, from house names to pub signs, has begun to be collected somewhere or other. A names society will have pointers, as well as references to journals and forthcoming conferences.

3 How to get involved with dictionaries

Join a dictionary society

Societies will keep you in touch with the latest trends, and provide information about resources, conferences, publications, and other events. In Europe there is the European Association for Lexicography: **http://www.euralex.org/**. In the US there is the Dictionary Society of North America: **http://polyglot.lss.wisc.edu/dsna/**. In the southern hemisphere, there is the Australasian Association for Lexicography: **http://www.australex.org/** and Afrilex, the African Association for lexicography: **http://www.up.ac.za/academic/libarts/afrilang/homelex.html**.

Subscribe to a journal

The main ones are the *International Journal of Lexicography*, also available online: **http://ijl.oxfordjournals.org/** and *Dictionaries*, the journal of the Dictionary Society of North America.

Send in words

Dictionary-compilers (*see* chapter 5) welcome assistance from everyone who can give evidence—which is you and me. If you want to contribute words, sources, and theories of origin to the OED Reading Programme, you can do so at: **http://www.oed.com/readers/research.html**. The page includes guidelines about how to become involved in dictionary research. A related information site is **http://www.askoxford.com/?view=uk**, especially the 'Ask the Experts' page.

Many dictionary publishers have 'wordwatch' sites, where you can be informed and often contribute at the same time. Here are a few.

Chambers:
http://www.chambersharrap.co.uk/chambers/features/wordwatch.php

Collins: **http://www.collins.co.uk/wordexchange/**

Longman: Wordwatch, in 2005 by post to Longman Dictionaries, Pearson Education, Edinburgh Gate, Harlow CM20 2JE.

Macmillan: **http://www.macmillandictionary.com/resourcenew.htm**

Merriam-Webster: **http://www.m-w.com/netdict.htm**

Explore a corpus

You can find out about the British National Corpus at: **http://www.natcorp.ox.ac.uk/**. Another site is the Longman/ Lancaster Corpus: **http://www.longman-elt.com/dictionaries/corpus/lclonlan.html**.

And for a wide range of references, go to this site, which is just as its domain suggests: **http://devoted.to/corpora**.

Read a book

Sydney Landau, *Dictionaries: the Art and Craft of Lexicography* (2nd edition, Cambridge University Press, 2001).

K.M. Elisabeth Murray, *Caught in the Web of Words* (Yale University Press, 1977).

Simon Winchester, *The Surgeon of Crowthorne* (Penguin, 1998) [*The Professor and the Madman* in the US] and *The Meaning of Everything* (Oxford University Press, 2003).

4 How to estimate the size of your vocabulary

i. Take a dictionary, any dictionary . . .

Take a medium-sized dictionary—one between 1,500 and 2,000 pages. Aim for a sample of pages which is 2 per cent of the whole. If the dictionary is 1,500 pages, that means a sample of thirty pages; 2,000 pages will give you forty. Ensure the sample is exactly 2 per cent, to make the final calculation easy (*see below*).

ii. Spread the sample

Break the sample down into a series of selections from different parts of the dictionary—say (for a thirty-page sample), six choices of five pages each, or ten choices of three pages. It isn't sensible to take all pages from a single part. If you chose letter U, for instance, you would find yourself flooded with words beginning with *un-*. But do make sure you include some prefixes. A representative sample would look like this: words beginning with CA-, EX-, JA-, OB-, PL-, SC-, TO-, and UN-.

iii. Check the words

Begin with the first full page in each case—in other words, if you are looking for EX- and you find a few EX- words at the bottom of page 467, ignore them and start at the top of 468.

Go through all the words on each page of your sample. Divide your page margins into two columns. (Alternatively, you can write the headwords out on a separate sheet of paper.) If you think you *know* a word, but would not use it yourself, put a light pencil tick in the left-hand column. If you think you would, in addition, actively *use* the word, put a tick in the right-hand column. This is the difference between your *passive* and *active* vocabulary (*see* p. 20). You may need to look at the definition or examples given next to the word before you can decide. Ignore the number of meanings the word has: if you know or use the word in *any* of its meanings, that will do.

In a more sophisticated version, you can have three columns under each of these headings. For passive vocabulary, you can ask yourself: 'Do I know the word well, vaguely, or not at all?' For active vocabulary, you can ask: 'Do I use the word often, occasionally, or not at all?' If you are uncertain, use the final column.

Make sure you don't miss any words out. Some dictionaries cluster (or 'nest') words together in bold face within an entry, just showing their endings, as in *nation*, *~al*, *~ize*. Don't ignore these. They are different words. Also include any phrases or idioms, such as *call up* and *call the tune*. Ignore alternative spellings: an example like *Caesarean/Cesarean* counts as just one word.

iv. Add up the ticks

Add up the ticks in each column, and jot the totals down at the bottom of each page. Then add up all the page totals. Multiply by 50 (if your sample was 2 per cent of the whole). The result will be, more or less, the size of your personal vocabulary.

The procedure, of course, doesn't allow for people who happen to know a large number of non-standard words, such as dialect words, which won't be in this kind of dictionary. And if you are, say, a scientist, it will underestimate your specialist vocabulary too. But the figure it gives will be an approximation of your everyday wordhoard. And it will be larger than you think (*see* chapter 3).

5 How to keep a record of your child's words

Keep a diary

Many parents keep a diary of their children's general development—when they sat up, crawled, cut a tooth, and so on. A diary of lexical development is no different, except that you need a bigger notebook. There are far more points of detail to be noted, and everything happens in such a short time. People talk of the 'milestones' of child development. In vocabulary, something interesting happens every few inches.

So, if you keep a lexical diary, it has to be very selective, otherwise it will quickly become voluminous. Most people restrict themselves to a list of notable words and anecdotes, written down when an opportunity arises. They usually start when a child approaches the 'first word' stage, around twelve months (*see* chapter 3) and last a year or so. But however long you keep the diary going for, it's well worth doing, and it's worth doing well. Some tips, therefore.

Make it sturdy

This is a book which is going to have a lot of use, being continually picked up and put down. Moreover, it gets put down in odd places, such as a bath or a bowl of porridge, so it needs to be quite tough if it is to survive. Choose a notebook with hard covers. Or an electronic one (but watch out for the bath). If you use electronic devices, such as a tape-recorder or a digital camera, make a regular back-up.

Remember the pencil

It may seem obvious, but you need something to write with. There is nothing worse than hearing a verbal gem and being unable to write it down because you can't find an unbroken pencil or a biro which works. By the time you've tracked one down, the gem can be forgotten or misremembered. Find a notebook with a pen(cil) attached, or tie one to the spine of the book. If you use a tape-recorder, always keep a spare tape.

Date things
Get into the habit of putting the date before each entry—and the age too, for ease of reference later. This is especially important if you decide to group the words thematically—words for clothes, words for cars, and so on. It's important too if the child is being brought up bilingually, and you decide to keep the words in the two languages in different places. With a tape-recorder, record the date on the tape as well as on the box.

'First words' provide the big opportunity for diary-keeping. When they start, expect to add new entries every couple of days. Remember to keep an eye on the situation in which a word is used. One day, the child may say *dog* pointing to a dog; the next day, pointing to a cat. You should make a note of the meanings as well.

Be accurate
Be as accurate as you can and write things down as soon as you can. There's not much point in writing down what you *think* the child said, several hours later. A language diary is different in this respect from a daily diary, which is often written up at the end of a person's day.

The biggest risk is that you write down things that the child has not actually said. *Kick ball* says the child, so you write down *Kick the ball*. The child says *doggie*, and you write *dog*. You have to train yourself to listen as carefully as you can, and be prepared for anything.

Don't expect to understand everything the child says. About a third of what children say in their second year isn't intelligible to anyone! Even older children can say things so fast or incoherently that it's not possible to be sure what was said.

Be unobtrusive

Don't draw attention to yourself as you write things down. Do it casually, and out of sight, if possible. Children get self-conscious at a very early age, as anyone knows who has tried to get them to talk into a tape-recorder. We don't want them to grow up thinking they are under permanent observation. Don't turn your interest into a regime. It shouldn't be: Big Mother is Watching You.

6 How to decide whether sounds have meanings

Test groups of words

Below you will find small groups of words with the same sound shape, and a suggestion as to what this shape conveys (*see* chapter 6). There are some examples which support this suggestion and some examples which do not. By collecting more instances, you can establish whether the hypotheses hold up for English. If you know other languages, you can look for similar sound structures there too.

Words beginning with *sl-*

These are supposed to convey downward movement, direction, or position.

To start you off: *slack, slide, slim, slope, slump*
Some exceptions: *sledge, sleek, slogan*

Words beginning with *sn-*

These are supposed to convey unpleasantness.

To start you off: *snag, snake, sneer, snipe, snout*
Some exceptions: *snooker, snow, snug*

Words beginning with *sw-*

These are supposed to convey smooth or wide-reaching movement.

To start you off: *swagger, swan, swat, swell, swoop*
Some exceptions: *swear, swine, switch*

Words beginning with *gl-*

These are supposed to convey brightness and light.

To start you off: *glamour, glare, gleam, glisten, glow*
Some exceptions: *gloom, glove, glue*

Becoming a word detective

Words ending in -*sh*
These are supposed to convey swift or strong movement.
   To start you off: *bash, crash, push, splash, whoosh*
   Some exceptions: *bush, wash, Welsh*

Words ending in -*p* preceded by a short vowel
These are supposed to convey suddenness or shortness.
   To start you off: *chop, drip, nip, stop, zap*
   Some exceptions: *cap, mop, ship*

Words ending in -*b* preceded by a short vowel
These are supposed to convey largeness, or lack of shape or direction.
   To start you off: *blob, club, grab, mob, slob*
   Some exceptions: *crib, job, lab*

7 How to get involved with dialects

Listen and note

The best examples of regional usage (*see* chapters 12 and 14) are around you in the street. Always have a notebook with you, and a pencil—better than a pen, as you can erase mistakes more easily. The notebook can, of course, be electronic, but this will let you down if you want to use some special marks or phonetic symbols.

Listen online

The BBC Voices project: **http://www.bbc.co.uk/voices/**

Accents and dialects in the British Library Sound Archive:
http://www.bl.uk/collections/sound-archive/accents.html

Collect Britain: **http://www.collectbritain.co.uk/collections/dialects/**

The Millennium Memory Bank:
http://www.bl.uk/collections/sound-archive/millenni.html

International Dialects of English Archive (mainly with actors in mind):
http://www.ku.edu/~idea/

Read a book or a journal

Jack Chambers and Peter Trudgill, *Dialectology* (Cambridge University Press, 1998).

Arthur Hughes and Peter Trudgill, *English Accents and Dialects* (Hodder Arnold, 1996).

Peter Trudgill, *The Dialects of England* (Blackwell, 1999).

American Speech: **http://www.dukeupress.edu/americanspeech/**

Dip into a dialect dictionary

The English Dialect Dictionary, edited by Joseph Wright (6 vols, Frowde, 1898).

Becoming a word detective

The Dictionary of American Regional English (Harvard University Press, since 1985).

The Concise Scots Dictionary, edited by Mairi Robinson (Aberdeen University Press, 1985).

Regional dictionaries include: *Australian National Dictionary* (1988), *Dictionary of South African English on Historical Principles* (1996), *Dictionary of New Zealand English* (1997), *Dictionary of Caribbean English Usage* (1996), all from Oxford University Press.

Find a relevant website

Many sites contain lists of dialect words and often audio clips. Type the name of an area plus the word *dialect* or *accent* into your search engine, and see. For example:

Lancashire: **http://www.nyt.co.uk/lancashire.htm**

Norfolk: **http://www.geocities.com/Heartland/Acres/5564/dialect.html**

Scotland:
http://www.scotsgate.com/dialeck.htm and **http://www.dsl.ac.uk/dsl/**

For global Englishes, the following sites are helpful:

South Africa: **http://www.ru.ac.za/affiliates/dsae/**

Australia: **http://www.anu.edu.au/ANDC/**

New Zealand:
http://www.oup.com.au/content/General.asp?ContentID=96&Master ID=48.

Join a society

North Country Dialect Societies at:
http://www.communigate.co.uk/ne/teesspeak/page27.phtml

Yorkshire Dialect Society: **http://www.clanvis.com/loc/dialect/**

American Dialect Society: **http://www.americandialect.org/**

And if there isn't one in your area: start one. Or set up a dialect blog.

8 How to find out more about words

Read more

If you like my own approach to words, and want to see more from the same pen, there is my *Cambridge Encyclopedia of the English Language* (Cambridge University Press, 2nd edition, 2003), *Stories of English* (Penguin, 2004), *Listen to Your Child* (Penguin, 1986), *Language Play* (Penguin, 1998), *Shakespeare's Words* (Penguin, 2002), and *The Shakespeare Miscellany* (Penguin, 2005), the last two co-authored with Ben Crystal.

For some of the other topics in this book:
Tony Augarde, *The Oxford Guide to Word Games* (OUP, 1984).

Ronald Carter, *Vocabulary* (Routledge, 1987).

Howard Jackson, *Words and their Meaning* (Longman, 1988).

Magnus Ljung, *Making Words in English* (Studentlitteratur, 2003).

Martin Manser, *The Guinness Book of Words* (Guinness Books, 1998).

Walter Nash, *Jargon* (Blackwell, 1993).

Randolph Quirk and Gabriele Stein, *English in Use* (Longman, 1990).

Walter Redfern, *Cliches and Coinages* (Blackwell, 1989) and *Puns* (Blackwell, 1984).

David Singleton, *Language and the Lexicon* (Arnold, 2000).

Gunnel Tottie, *An Introduction to American English* (Blackwell, 2002).

More detailed sources for all the quotations in this book, and many more besides, are found in *Words on Words* (Penguin, 2000), co-authored with Hilary Crystal.

Becoming a word detective

Find a website
Not a difficult task. There are hundreds. Here are a few:

World Wide Words: **http://www.worldwidewords.org/index.htm**

Allwords: **http://www.allwords.com/**

Wordsmith: **http://www.wordsmith.org**

The Word Detective: **http://www.word-detective.com/**

And, for those wanting to improve their Anglo-Saxon skills, there is the Wikipedia Old English website:
http://ang.wikipedia.org/wiki/H%C3%A9afods%C3%ADde

Subscribe to a journal
The quarterly *English Today* (Cambridge University Press) covers all varieties of national and international English: see **http://uk.cambridge.org/journals**. Information about *Verbatim*, also a quarterly, is at **http://www.verbatimmag.com**.

Join a society
There may be a club or society for wordsmiths in your area. If not, start one.

Answers

Answers to panel on p. 15

Name	Associated meaning
Broadway	theatre world
Number 10	UK government
Madison Avenue	advertising
Bollywood	films
Fleet Street	newspaper publishing
Old Bailey	justice
Harley Street	medicine
Fort Knox	security
Dartmoor	prison
Scotland Yard	policing

Note that the meaning can survive, even if the 'real world' changes. Fleet Street in London is no longer the centre of the British newspaper world.

Answers to panel on p. 89

-os: *armadillo, casino, inferno, photo, proviso, solo, zero*
-oes: *echo, embargo, hero, mosquito, tomato, torpedo, veto*
-os or *-oes*: *cargo, ghetto, memento, volcano*

Index of subjects

Index of subjects

language police 129
Latin 43–4, 98, 110
   loanwords 50–52, 63
lawyers 63
learning disabilities 24
learning words 25–32
lexemes 17
lexicographers 33, 151
lexicography 33–40
lexicology 3, 6–8
lipograms 180–1
literary vocabulary 186
literature 183–6
loaded words 128–30
loanwords 50–63, 86, 110–12, 157
London Underground stations 169
longest words 64–5
ludic linguistics 176

malapropisms 174
Meaning of Liff, The 47, 79
mobility 94–6

name societies 191
names, *see* proper names
narrowing of meaning 152
new Englishes 106–11
New Oxford Dictionary of English, The 66
newspaper headlines 175
nicknames 74
noun plurals 102–3
novels 161
nuances 128

occupational dialects 116
offensive words 130
Old English 50, 98
onomastics 79, 191

onomatopoeia 45–9
opposites 29
order of words 98–9
origins:
   of language 45, 48
   of words 41–80
orthoepists 84, 86
Outline of English Speech-Craft, An 50
Oxford Dictionary of Quotations, The 34
Oxford English Dictionary, The 10, 50, 65, 117, 138–41, 144, 189

parts of speech 70–1
passive vocabulary 20–22
phonaesthetics 171
ping-pong punning 172–3
place names 76, 191–2
Plain English Campaign 120–21
playing with language 172–6
playing with words 165–86
poetry 184
   competitions 159–60
political correctness 128–30
political language 122
popular etymology 61
portmanteau words 69
power of words 4
prefixes 64–7
prescriptive grammar 37
primitive languages 22
printing 85
proper names 12–13, 72–9, 191–3
proverbs 4–5
puns 172
purr words 127

Queen's English, The 156

Index of people

Index of people

Index of words

This index lists words which have been used as a main illustration or focus of discussion in the book.

Index of words